HOUDINI
MASTER OF ILLUSION

HOUDINI
MASTER OF ILLUSION

CLINTON COX

scholastic press • new york

All rights reserved. Published by Scholastic
Press, a division of Scholastic Inc., *Publishers
since 1920.* SCHOLASTIC and SCHOLASTIC PRESS
and associated logos are trademarks and/or reg-
istered trademarks of Scholastic Inc.

Library of Congress Cataloging-in Publication
Data Cox, Clinton Houdini /
by Clinton Cox. p.cm.

ISBN 0-590-94960-8

1. Houdini, Harry, 1874-1926--Juvenile litera-
ture. 2. Magicians--United States--Biography--
Juvenile literature. 3. Escape artists--United
States--Biography--Juvenile literature. [1.
Houdini, Harry, 1874-1926. 2. Magicians.] I.
Title. GV1545.H8 C69 2001   793.8'092-
dc21 [B]   00-052673

10 9 8 7 6 5 4 3 2 1   01 02 03 04 05

Printed in U.S.A.   37
First edition, September 2001

The display type was set in Helvetica 25
Ultra Thin, Helvetica 35 Thin and
Comenius Antiqua. The text type
was set in Cochin 13-point.

Book design by Yvette Awad

Picture research
Zoe Moffit

To my nieces
and nephews:
Katie, Jessica,
Maggie Mae,
Jamie and
Jeremy Boyd,
and Dylan Parker.
May you always
believe this is a
magical world.

INTRODUCTION

Harry Houdini was the most famous escape artist and magician the world has ever known.

Performing during what has been called the Golden Age of Magic, he escaped from chains wrapped around his body and fastened by several locks. He walked out of locked jail cells built to hold the most violent men, and freed himself from a dreaded "transport cell" wagon used to carry Russian convicts to Siberia.

With thousands of spectators watching in New York, Chicago, and other cities, he freed himself from straitjackets while hanging upside down from the edge of skyscrapers.

His magic tricks included many performed by other magicians, but he also developed some that had never been done before: walking through a brick wall and making an elephant disappear.

His deeds seemed so impossible that spectators

said he must have used supernatural means to accomplish them. Houdini always denied this and even explained how many of the tricks were done, but the aura of mystery that surrounded him remained no matter what he said.

He became a figure of legend and myth well before his death in 1926, and remains such a figure today.

Irish writer James Joyce referred to him in his classic 1939 novel, *Finnegans Wake*, when he wrote of "escape master-in-chief from all sorts of houdingplaces." And E. L. Doctorow's best-selling 1975 novel, *Ragtime*, featured Houdini as a major character.

The word *Houdini* is routinely used to describe anyone who performs an incredible deed, especially if it involves escaping from a situation that seems impossible. Though time has diminished the fame of most of the people who were household names when Houdini was alive, it has only increased his fame and the legend that surrounds it.

Harry Houdini was a remarkable man who seemed obsessed with proving that the world had never seen anyone like him before and would never see his like again.

His fame today is a tribute to how well he succeeded in rising from a poverty-stricken background to become, as fans often called him because of his seemingly impossible feats, "the man who walked through walls."

one

Although he claimed all his life that he was born in Appleton, Wisconsin, Harry Houdini was born in Budapest, Hungary, in 1874.

His father, Mayer Samuel Weiss, and his mother, Cecilia Steiner Weiss, named him Ehrich. He was one of six children to survive to adulthood in the desperately poor family. At least two other siblings died at an early age.

"Such hardships and hunger became our lot," he recalled years later, "that the less said on the subject the better."

The family moved to the United States and settled in Appleton in 1876. After he became famous, Houdini always told reporters his father was a distinguished rabbi — a teacher of the Jewish religion — and a lawyer.

Like much of what Houdini claimed about himself and his family in later years, though, it is hard to separate fact from fiction. Although his father was a religious scholar and teacher, there is no proof that he was ever admitted to the bar or formally ordained as a rabbi. A small congregation in Appleton, however, chose him to serve as its rabbi at a salary that barely kept the family alive. But after four years the congregation replaced him with a younger man, and the family moved to Milwaukee.

The fifty-three-year-old Mayer Weiss (twelve years older than his wife) was unable to find work and Houdini's mother was forced to appeal to the Hebrew Relief Society for fuel and food.

All of the sons began helping out as soon as they were old enough to work. At the age of eight, Ehrich began selling the *Milwaukee Journal* on the street and also shined shoes.

Whether to escape the poverty of his family or because he was seeking adventure, Ehrich ran away from home the day after his twelfth birthday by hopping a freight train. His exact wanderings are not clear, but he was away for about a year.

While he was gone, his father moved to New York City and tried to make a living as a rabbi. As in Appleton, however, he met with failure in the role he loved so much and finally found work in a necktie-cutting factory.

Ehrich joined his father in 1887, and also began working at the factory. By saving every penny they could, father and son finally managed to reunite the family in a tiny apartment in Manhattan. Money was still scarce, however, and at one point Mayer Weiss was forced to sell one of his most treasured possessions, a set of *The Codes of Maimonides*. The *Codes* are a code of Jewish law written by Maimonides, a medieval Jewish philosopher, jurist, and physician.

A rabbi named Bernard Drachman had offered to give Weiss money, but the proud man insisted on giving Rabbi Drachman the set in return.

"We lived there, I mean starved there, several years," Houdini wrote of the family's early years in New York.

There are many stories about how he first became interested in magic. According to one tale told by Houdini, he was a child prodigy who was so good at mastering locks that a professional locksmith employed him. In another, he said he learned how to pick locks as a child in order to break into his mother's pie cabinet. The truth is that Houdini did not learn how to master locks until he was an adult.

Yet another story told by Houdini was that he was hired by a traveling circus when he was nine years old to perform an act he had originated: hanging upside down from a trapeze while picking up pins with his eyelids.

That would have been quite an accomplishment for an adult, much less a child. In reality, young Ehrich learned his first magic trick in New York while working as a photographer's assistant (probably at 15 or 16, but the exact age is uncertain). The photographer was an amateur magician and taught Houdini and his brother Theo how to make a coin vanish.

Ehrich's interest in magic quickly grew. Together with a fellow necktie-factory worker named Jacob "Jake" Hyman, Ehrich began performing at local boys' clubs and other small places.

He billed himself as "Eric the Great," and his tricks were performed mainly with cards and pieces of silk, because those objects were the only ones he could afford.

He also began two other activities as a young teenager that would serve him well in the years ahead: speaking in public at amateur theatricals, and swimming, diving, and running track at the Pastime Athletic Club.

A photograph of him at the time shows him wearing a few medals he won, and several more he borrowed or bought so he would look more impressive.

Many of the escapes that would later make him famous depended on the physical strength he began building as a youngster.

One evening on his way home from work, Ehrich bought a battered secondhand book for ten cents: *The Memoirs of Robert-Houdin, Ambassador, Author, and Conjuror, Written by Himself*. It was a book that would change Ehrich's life.

"From the moment I began to study the art he became my guide and my hero," he wrote years later. "I asked nothing more of life than to become in my profession like Robert-Houdin."

Robert-Houdin was a French clerk, originally named Jean Eugene Robert, who had studied, practiced, and performed until he became famous throughout the world as the Father of Modern Magic.

Young Ehrich became obsessed with Robert-Houdin's life. Here was someone who had done what he dreamed of doing: gained fame, fortune, and the acceptance of people in all walks of life by performing magic tricks onstage.

Ehrich had always been determined to succeed,

but now that determination governed his life. He practiced sleight-of-hand tricks for hours at a time. More important for the future Harry Houdini, though, were the strenuous escapes he practiced day after day on the roof of the family tenement.

To the bewilderment of his mother and father, Ehrich would have his brother Theodore (nicknamed "Dash") tie him with ropes. Then Ehrich would spend hours freeing himself.

In 1891, at the age of seventeen, Ehrich felt confident enough to quit his job at the necktie factory to become a full-time magician. His mother is said to have reacted to this move by asking in disbelief, "*Nu*, so from this you should make a living, my son?"

Ehrich did not look like the public's ideal of a stage performer. He was only about five feet five inches tall, and was reportedly given to sprinkling his sentences with "youse" and "ain't" (his mother and father spoke mostly German, so Ehrich learned his English on the streets).

But he already possessed the traits so many people would talk about in the years to come: an unshakeable belief in his destiny, the courage to try virtually anything, and a smile and stage presence that captivated audiences.

Thanks to his friend, Jacob Hyman, Ehrich Weiss was also now the proud possessor of a new name: Harry Houdini. The "Harry" part was probably an Americanization of his nickname, Ehrie, but "Houdini" was Hyman's suggestion.

Hyman told him that the French added an *i* to a word to make it mean "like," so that "Houdini" would mean "like Houdin," and make him instantly recognizable in the world of magic.

So Ehrich Weiss, the son of a Jewish scholar who yearned for his son to follow in his footsteps, was now Harry Houdini, budding magician. Houdini never said publicly what his father thought about his decision.

Harry and Theodore billed themselves as the Brothers Houdini and wore costumes their mother made from pieces of silk the boys managed to find. They performed at beer halls, neighborhood gatherings, fraternal meetings, and anywhere else people were willing to pay a few dollars.

Houdini's father looked on in bewilderment at the path his son had chosen to follow and never saw him perform. Worn down by years of struggle, Mayer Weiss died in 1892 after undergoing surgery for cancer of the tongue. He had known nothing but poverty in the nation he had moved to sixteen years earlier, and on his deathbed made Ehrich promise to look after his mother no matter what happened. It was a promise the youth gladly gave, for the strong bond between mother and son would last all his life.

Houdini said he remembered his mother crying out in German when his father died: "Weiss, Weiss, you've left me with your children! What have you done?"

The grinding poverty his family had always known gave Houdini a determination to succeed that would later be called superhuman by the people who knew him. In the years to come, faced by obstacles that would have made almost anyone else give up, he threw his energy into finding ways to go around or through them.

Now, with his father gone and the family poorer than ever, Houdini promised his mother he would one day pour gold coins into her lap.

It was a promise he would keep.

two

The year after his father died, Houdini performed in the Columbian Exposition at the Chicago World's Fair with his brother Theo. The fair was the biggest show in the history of the nation, and celebrated the four-hundredth anniversary of the arrival of Christopher Columbus to the Americas.

Performers traveled to the fair from all over the United States and from foreign countries. One of the main attractions was a mile-long midway that included replicas of an Eskimo village and a South Sea Islands village; performances by the great pianist, Ignace Paderewski; and the world's first Ferris wheel, George Ferris's 264-foot "bicycle-in-the-sky."

Houdini gained valuable experience here, and also apparently learned a trick at the fair that would become part of his routine for the rest of his life. A fellow magician taught him how to "swallow" a mouthful of needles and thread, then bring them back out of his mouth with the needles threaded.

After appearing at the fair, Houdini was booked as a solo act in a "dime museum." At the end of the nineteenth century, dime museums were the cheapest form of entertainment offered to the public. The museums featured sword swallowers, contortionists, fire-eaters, people who were unusually short or tall or deformed in some way, and other acts meant to attract the curious.

Houdini performed as many as twenty shows a day for twelve dollars a week. He kept only about two dollars a week for himself and sent the rest to his mother.

His act consisted of a few card tricks, producing a handerkerchief from the flame of a candle, and a trick he and his brother called "Metamorphosis."

Metamorphosis was a variation on a "box" trick magicians had performed for years. In his version, Houdini tied Theo's hands behind his back with a rope, then put him in a sack, which Houdini tied at the top. The sack was then placed in a trunk, which was locked and tied with ropes.

Houdini placed a cabinet ten to twelve feet wide and about seven feet high between the trunk and the audience. The cabinet had a curtain Houdini closed so no one could see the trunk. Then he told the audience, "When I clap my hands three times — behold a miracle!"

Unknown to the audience, the trunk contained a secret panel that could be opened from the inside with a special device, allowing one person to exit without disturbing the lock or ropes, and another person to enter.

Stepping behind the curtain, Houdini clapped three times and out stepped Theo. Almost immediately, Theo ducked behind the curtain, unlocked the trunk and out stepped Houdini, his body bound with ropes just as Theo's had been.

The trick required incredible agility by both participants in order to be successful, and the Brothers Houdini possessed that agility.

"Just think over this," Houdini boasted in an advertisement. "The time consumed in making the change is THREE SECONDS!" Houdini would use the Metamorphosis trick for the rest of his career, often introducing changes to keep the trick fresh.

Back in New York, the brothers still performed at lodge meetings, neighborhood gatherings, and in beer halls in Manhattan.

The beer halls were so packed with tables that there was barely room for the waiters to walk. The noisy crowds were more interested in drinking than in watching performers, and there were so many fights most people simply ignored them. It was a rough place for a young performer, but it helped give Houdini valuable experience.

One day the Brothers Houdini were hired by the panicky manager of the Imperial Theater after his opening act failed to show up. They lasted just one performance, however. Houdini placed Theo inside the trunk, pulled the curtain, and declared, "When I clap my hands three times — behold a miracle!"

He then ducked behind the curtain and the audience waited expectantly, but nothing happened. Houdini discovered that Theo could not get out of the trunk because he had left the device to open the secret panel back in the dressing room.

The manager fired them, and from then on it was Houdini who was locked in the trunk and Theo who cried, "Behold a miracle!"

In the spring of 1894 the brothers began performing at Brooklyn's Coney Island. In an incident that had a profound influence on his career and became part of the Houdini mythology, a manager reportedly called him aside one day and asked, "Harry, why do you say, 'Ladies and Gents, as youse can see I ain't got nothing up my sleeve?'"

"Because I ain't," Houdini replied. "What's the matter with what I say?"

"Nothing," the manager replied. "Except that it's bad grammar to say 'ain't.'"

Whether the incident happened exactly that way or not, Houdini reportedly never said "ain't" again onstage. Scholar's son that he was, he remained extremely sensitive throughout his life about his lack of formal education, and never stopped trying to impress people with the knowledge he gained from almost constant reading. (Decades later, when listed in *Who's Who* as a "magician," he asked the editors to change the listing to "actor, inventor, and author.")

The Brothers Houdini act came to an end less than two months after they opened at Coney Island. The cause was an eighteen-year-old, ninety-four-pound woman named Wilhelmina Beatrice Rahner.

"Bess," as Houdini called her the rest of his life, was half of a song-and-dance act called the Floral Sisters. There are several versions of how they met, with Houdini telling one story, Bess another, and Theo yet a third.

Theo said he dated her first, then introduced her to his brother. Bess said they met when Houdini spilled water on her dress while he was performing at a school in Brooklyn. Houdini said they met when he dropped some equipment on her while riding on a streetcar.

Whichever version is correct, the couple had a whirlwind romance and were married in a civil ceremony on June 22, 1894, less than a month after they met. Bess said their honeymoon, which was in Coney Island, was "cheap, but glorious."

In an attempt to please their families, Houdini and Bess were married twice more, before a rabbi and a priest.

"I'm the most married person I know," Bess said. "Three times, and to the same man."

Bess's widowed mother, a German Catholic, was so furious with her daughter for marrying a Jew that she refused to speak to her. But Houdini's mother, Cecilia, welcomed the young couple into her home.

"It was a poor and crowded home," Bess said. "In fact, for that first night, there was really no room for us."

The couple would live with Houdini's mother for the remaining nineteen years of her life, whenever they weren't on the road. But it took Bess's mother another twelve years to accept Houdini.

"I was seriously ill and wanted her badly," Bess said of the eventual reconciliation with her mother, "so Houdini, with one of his brothers, went to her home and would not leave until she came to me. Thereafter he was the same as a son to her."

Houdini said that his marriage to Bess "brought me luck and it has been with me ever since. I never had any before I married her."

Bess soon joined Houdini as part of the act. Theo, adopting the stage name of Professor Houdini and later Hardeen, went off on his own.

Houdini jokingly referred to Bess as "my large wife." Her tiny size made her ideal for rapidly changing places with him in the box during the Metamorphosis trick.

The two were booked into dime museums in Virginia, then headed to New York City to perform at Huber's Palace Museum. Other acts at Huber's included Count Orloff, the "Human Window Pane" (YOU CAN SEE HIS HEART BEAT! YOU CAN SEE HIS BLOOD CIRCULATE! read the advertisement); Thardo, a woman who let herself be bitten repeatedly by a rattlesnake; Unthan, a man with no arms who could play the violin with his toes; performing monkeys; and a sprinting contest for fat ladies.

Houdini tried to make some extra money by selling a booklet he wrote titled *Mysterious Harry Houdini: Tricks Requiring no practice or special apparatus*.

Apparently several people bought the booklet, for in the diary he began keeping at this time, he wrote: "Graft Big."

Harry and Bess performed as many as fourteen shows a day. It was valuable experience for both, but Bess was sometimes so depressed by the surroundings that she refused to appear.

Beginning in the spring of 1895, they toured for six months with the small Welsh Brothers Circus in Pennsylvania. Bess sang and danced. In addition to his magic tricks, Harry did the Punch-and-Judy show with puppets he had carved with a jackknife, using his face as the model. He also played Projea, the Wild Man of Mexico, fashioning a costume out of old sacks.

One day he was hit in the eye by a piece of raw meat someone threw in his cage, and his eye was swollen shut for three weeks.

The finale of their performance was always Metamorphosis, and it never failed to excite the audience. The suddenness of their switch in the trunk, wrote a reporter in one newspaper, left the audience "almost too astonished to applaud."

"Our act is the supreme cabinet mystery in the World," Houdini wrote in an advertisement that showed little regard for the truth. "[It] has been featured at . . . the Oxford London and has created a sensation in Europe, Australia, and America."

During this time Houdini also laid the foundation for becoming the greatest escape artist the world has ever known.

He began collecting handcuffs and spent countless hours learning the secrets of locksmiths. He discovered that most handcuffs were far easier to open than the public thought. Though made by different manufacturers, almost all were built the same way and could be opened with the same key.

He also discovered that it was possible to open many handcuffs simply by rapping them sharply on a certain spot, or by inserting a thin piece of wire or steel in them.

Perhaps most important of all during his tour with the circus, however, Houdini learned where to hide a key or piece of metal where no one would dream of looking: down his throat.

This knowledge was taught to him by an old Japanese man who was a member of a balancing troupe. The man was also an expert at swallowing objects so they couldn't be seen, even when people looked in his mouth, then bringing the objects back up.

He taught Houdini how to swallow a solid ivory

ball, then regurgitate it. At first Houdini practiced with a small peeled potato tied to the end of a string. He sometimes failed to bring the potato back up, but no harm was done because it simply slid down into his stomach and was digested.

Practicing constantly in his spare time during the next few weeks, Harry soon was able to swallow and retrieve the ivory ball, an ability that would prove invaluable in the years ahead.

During this time he also practiced improving his speech and delivery, trying to overcome the lack of formal education that had led him to say "ain't" and "youse."

He was so determined to improve himself and his act that he kept a notebook beside his bed for jotting down ideas that came to him in the middle of the night. In the morning, after five hours of sleep at the most, he would immediately begin working on the new ideas.

He continued to learn everything he could about handcuffs, buying several different kinds and getting to the point where he could escape from three pairs at once. Handcuff escapes were still a minor part of his act, however.

Bess said he was so focused on developing new

ideas for the act that he often forgot to eat or change his clothes. Sometimes she stole his underwear during the night and replaced it with a clean pair. Otherwise, she said, he would have gone on wearing the same old pair without ever thinking about it.

One Sunday the show opened in a small town in Rhode Island, even though the state had a law against Sunday amusements. The sheriff arrested the entire cast, including Harry and Bess, and locked them in jail overnight. Harry was appalled, fearful of the disgrace he had brought on his father's name, and afraid of the effect the news might have on his mother.

Even though the arrest was for a petty offense, it remained one of his most closely guarded secrets for years. When he finally talked about it publicly, he used it to add to the Houdini myth. As soon as the jailer left, he claimed in later years, he borrowed a hatpin from Bess, picked the lock, and freed all the performers. The truth was that he and the other performers remained in jail until the owner bailed them out.

During his time with the circus, Harry sent half the twenty-five dollars he made a week to his mother. He added to his income by selling soap, toothpaste, and other items to his fellow performers, and managed to build up a small nest egg.

Houdini used the money to buy a half share in the American Gaiety Girls, a small traveling burlesque show. The show, he boasted, was "the finest, cleanest, and largest show of its kind on the road . . ."

One reviewer who saw the Gaiety Girls, however, wrote: "Many portions of the dialogue and much of the stage business is vulgar, and some of it positively indecent in tenor and allusion."

Harry and Bess were billed as "European Illusionists," and also doubled as singers and dancers. One of the other acts was Wrestling May Morgan, who took on all comers, both male and female. May Morgan was also the wife of the company's business manager.

When it came to generating publicity, Harry possessed a brilliance few performers have matched. He knew that people were fascinated by challenges, especially ones hurled at authorities, and what better authority figures to challenge than the police?

Before the Gaiety Girls' first appearance in Woonsocket, Rhode Island, he dropped by the local police station and asked to be restrained by six pairs of handcuffs at once. He then hurried into a private room and returned in less than a minute with all the cuffs opened.

Newspapermen loved the stunt, which he repeated in Worcester and Holyoke, Massachusetts. It gave him the free publicity he was looking for, but the Gaiety Girls' needed more than free publicity. The company collapsed, unable to pay its railroad fares or employee salaries. Wrestling May Morgan was charged with fraud and her husband was also arrested.

Harry and Bess joined a small magic show called the Marco Company, and began touring the Canadian province of Nova Scotia.

In Halifax, Houdini came up with another idea for free publicity. He advertised that he would escape in full view of spectators while roped, handcuffed, and shackled on the back of a "wild horse."

It was a potentially brilliant idea, but the horse refused to cooperate. Unnerved by Houdini's wriggling on his back, the horse took off. By the time he stopped from exhaustion, he and his passenger were miles away. Houdini managed to free himself, but only the horse saw him do it.

A few days later in the town of New Brunswick, a doctor took Houdini along on a call to an insane asylum. There Houdini saw an inmate rolling on the floor as he desperately tried to free himself from a leather and canvas straitjacket.

The doctor told Houdini it was impossible for anyone to escape once bound, but Houdini saw the jacket as a challenge. Using a straitjacket given to him by the doctor, he practiced for a week and then successfully performed the escape in front of an audience for the first time.

The Marco Company soon folded, and for the next two years Harry and Bess roamed the Northeast and Midwest looking for work and finding only the lowest-paying jobs.

"In those early job-seeking days I was sometimes more of a handicap than an asset," Bess said. "I was a frail little thing . . . Once, when work was scarce in both dime museums and halls, and we tried almost despairingly to break into a burlesque show, the manager took one disgusted glance at me and cried, 'What the hell d'you think I'm running? A kindergarten?'"

In one show Houdini worked as "Cardo," performing card tricks. Another time he was "Professor Murat," a hypnotist. Bess was billed as "The Melodious Little Songster." In Chicago, trying to scrape together a few dollars by gambling, Houdini lost sixty dollars.

He was booked by chance into a show in Appleton, and returned there for the first time in fifteen years. The local newspaper lauded him as "Mr. Weiss, the magician," and Houdini told the reporter he had performed in England and "studied and practiced for a considerable time in London."

The winter of 1897 found Harry and Bess stranded in St. Louis without work or money. With one dollar fifty cents he somehow managed to scrape up, Harry rented a small bedroom for a week. Then he used his sleight-of-hand ability to steal six potatoes from a grocer.

On the way home, he found a large wooden packing case someone had thrown away and took it back to the bedroom. There he split it apart and used the pieces to build a fire to cook the potatoes and warm himself and Bess.

Almost anyone else would have been ready to quit, but Harry was as convinced as ever that he would be famous. One day he found work at a local music hall by claiming to be a comedian. Then he hurriedly visited several barbershops, read the jokes in their old humor magazines, and put together a comedy routine.

Bess sang songs in her high-pitched, little girl's voice and Harry dressed as a tramp and told old jokes. To their surprise, the audience loved them. They were held over for three weeks, but at the end of that time were once more out of work.

Worn out from the constant scramble for work, Harry and Bess were glad to sign on with Dr. Thomas Hill's California Concert Company, a traveling medicine show playing small towns in Kansas. They were paid twenty-five dollars a week, plus board and traveling expenses.

"Dr. Hill" had long brown hair and a flowing beard, and an ability to make people believe his worthless bottles of "medicine" could cure all kinds of ailments. He sold the bottles on street corners, then urged people to attend the show at night. The shows were usually given in tents or on outdoor stages.

Harry and Bess were billed as the "Great Wizard" and the "Little Vocalist." Seeking to attract bigger crowds, Dr. Hill asked Harry to present a spirit show on Sundays, complete with fake mind readings and effects such as bells ringing when no one seemed to be touching them, trumpets flying through the air, tambourines jangling, the dead talking, and other mysterious happenings.

Spiritualism was widely popular at the turn of the century, with people from all walks of life believing it was possible to communicate with the dead. At gatherings they held called séances, spiritualists claimed that the effects people saw and heard were produced by their dead loved ones.

When Dr. Hill asked Harry to do the spirit show, he quickly agreed, especially after Hill offered him a salary increase and top billing as "Houdini the Great."

ONLY TIME A SÉANCE IN PUBLIC EVER GIVEN BY HOUDINI, the posters advertised, EXCEPT IN LARGE CITIES AND THEN AT ADVANCED PRICES.

The show drew packed audiences in town after town. After one show, Harry eagerly wrote in his diary, "Broke the record at Garnet for paid admissions. Spiritualism cause of it — bad effect — 1034 Paid Admission to see spiritualism."

The "bad effect" was apparently the guilty conscience he suffered from tricking people into believing their loved ones were communicating with them.

Dr. Hill's California Concert Company soon folded, and Harry and Bess returned for another six months with the Welsh Brothers Circus.

Metamorphosis was now used as the climax of the circus's performances for the first time, and Harry was allowed to make his handcuff escapes an important part of the act. He also began building up his body for the strength that was essential for the future escapes he had in mind. Every day he ran a mile or two, rode a bicycle, and worked out on a horizontal bar with an acrobatic troupe.

By the fall of 1898, though, he was tired of the circus and wrote in his diary, "Last two weeks seemed like eternity."

Harry was now twenty-four years old and had been performing for seven years. But despite all his efforts, the agents he depended on to give him bookings still thought of him as "Dime Museum Harry."

He and Bess returned to New York, where they moved in with his mother. He sent out flyers advertising a program for the coming year that would "reflect credit on any house we may be booked at."

There was so little interest in the act that he put together a sixteen-page catalog for Harry Houdini's School of Magic. He offered to sell the magic secrets it had taken him so long to learn, and the books on magic he had spent years collecting.

"Do you believe in Spiritualism?" he wrote. "If not, why not? . . . I can give you full instructions and make you a full-fledged medium."

He even offered to sell the most valuable parts of his act: Metamorphosis, "The Greatest Novelty

Mystery Act in the World! (price on application)," and the secrets of his handcuff escapes.

"You defy the police authorities and sheriffs to place handcuffs or leg shackles on you, and can easily escape. Price on application."

Despairing of ever breaking out of the grinding, low-paying world of dime museums, beer halls, circuses, and medicine shows, Harry told Bess he was almost ready to quit.

By the end of 1898, he wrote years later, he had become so discouraged "that I contemplated quitting the show business . . . meaning to work by day at one of my trades . . . and open a school of magic."

He gave himself a deadline of one year to succeed. Though there was no way he could have known it as he met rejection after rejection, 1899 would finally launch him on the success he had dreamed of as a child.

three

Harry's discouragement did not last long. By the first week in January 1899, he was in Chicago challenging the police to lock him in handcuffs and leg irons.

In his previous challenges to police, he had simply walked into station houses and introduced himself, hoping that reporters would learn of his successful escapes. Sometimes they did and sometimes they didn't.

As usual, Harry learned from his failures. In Chicago he had his manager introduce him to several local reporters, who in turn made sure he met a detective named Andy Rohan. While Bess kept Rohan engaged in conversation, Harry examined the locks on the cell doors.

That night he made a pick that would open all the cell doors. The next day, accompanied by reporters, Harry returned to challenge Rohan.

The detective fastened three pairs of handcuffs on him, then locked him in a cell. Harry was free within minutes, but when he walked out the reporters weren't impressed: They said he had probably made a duplicate key of the locks.

Harry was furious and challenged them to strip him naked, search him, and lock him up again. While Bess left the room, the reporters did just that. This time Harry freed himself even faster than before. The result was all he had hoped for: a feature story complete with a photograph on the front page of the Chicago *Journal*.

Harry hurried back to his hotel with several copies of the paper, burst into his room, and shouted, "Bess we've made it! I'm famous!"

He was not famous yet, but he cut out the article for his scrapbook and wrote next to it: "first time my Picture ever appeared in a newspaper."

The free publicity resulted in an offer of star billing at a local theater, which he quickly accepted. A week later, however, Harry suffered one of the worst humiliations of his career.

In response to his challenge, a big man came onstage and snapped a pair of handcuffs on him. Harry stepped behind the curtain and tried to open the cuffs with his duplicate key. Try as he might, however, the cuffs refused to open.

Finally the stranger, who turned out to be a policeman, told him he had dropped birdshot into the lock and the cuffs would have to be sawed off.

It had never occurred to Harry that anyone would deliberately ruin a good pair of handcuffs. At first he was astonished, then angry. Throughout his life he would rarely forgive or forget a wrong, whether it was real or one he imagined, and he never forgot or forgave the policeman who tricked him.

But as usual he learned from the experience: From that day on he never allowed anyone to lock handcuffs on him until he made sure they worked.

The vaudeville theaters Harry longed to break into hosted the most popular entertainment in the country, and were the best-paying for performers. There were approximately two thousand vaudeville houses in the country, with the majority controlled by just two chains: the Keith circuit in the East and the Orpheum circuit in the West.

A few weeks after appearing in Chicago, Harry performed in a beer hall in St. Paul, Minnesota. There he suddenly received the break he had been waiting for.

One night his performance was watched by a group of visiting theater managers, including a short, heavyset man who spoke with a thick German accent. The man doubted that the handcuffs Harry escaped from were legitimate, so he "purchased a few pairs and sent them onstage," Harry remembered years later.

The stranger was so impressed with Houdini's ease in escaping from them that he invited him to dinner. There he finally introduced himself: Martin Beck, head of the Orpheum circuit.

Beck urged Harry to eliminate most of the magic acts he was doing and concentrate on the handcuff escapes and Metamorphosis. A few days later Harry received a telegram from Beck that read, "You can open Omaha March twenty-sixth sixty dollars, will see act probably make you proposition for all next season."

Harry wrote across the bottom of the telegram, which he kept for the rest of his life, "This wire changed my whole Life's journey."

Beck's insistence on highlighting the escape acts was brilliant. The combination of escapes and the successful challenges Harry issued to the police and his audience brought wild applause in city after city.

He made at least one challenge at every performance, daring someone in the audience to place their own handcuffs on him. By now Harry possessed both an encyclopedic knowledge of locks, and duplicate keys or metal picks that could open most locks.

He would claim later in his career that his memory was so good he had only to glance at a key to be able to make a duplicate of it (the mystery still remains, however, of where he hid the scores of keys he needed, and how he could quickly find the right one for a particular lock).

To make sure someone would respond to his challenges, Harry also paid men to sit in the audience. If no one else volunteered, one of them would rush onstage with a pair of handcuffs he had given them.

His performance in Omaha was so popular that Beck raised his salary and signed him to do the entire Orpheum circuit. By the time Harry and Bess reached San Francisco, he was making ninety dollars a week, which was almost one fifth the money the average American family earned in a year.

"I have laid out the plan for you very carefully," Beck told him. "My aim especially is at present to make a name for you."

The name was now being made. In San Francisco, an English magician calling himself Professor Benzon wrote an article saying Harry escaped by having "conveniently about him all keys known to the handcuff trade."

The charge was probably true, but Harry called it "absurdly simple," and offered to perform a handcuff escape at the police station. In order to make sure he had no hidden keys on his body, he said, he would perform the escape almost nude.

After stripping before a crowd of police officials and patrolmen, a police surgeon and two assistants examined him. They even taped his mouth shut and searched between his toes.

Detectives locked his hands behind his back with four types of handcuffs, put two pairs of leg irons on him, then joined the hand and leg shackles together with yet another pair of handcuffs.

"This brought him to a crouching posture," wrote a local reporter, "and made him to all appearances helpless to use a key even if he had one."

The detectives then placed Harry inside a closet, which they had previously searched. Ten minutes later he walked out. The spectators could not believe it when they saw all the manacles lying on the closet floor, still locked.

"The Naked Test" became a regular part of Harry's publicity campaigns, which he repeated in police stations in city after city (he was not actually naked, which would not have been allowed, but wore a brief loincloth). The test never failed to garner publicity, and Houdini mailed hundreds of copies of newspaper articles about himself to agents, theaters, and magazines throughout the country.

"Your clippings is what gets you the engagements," Beck advised him.

"Who created the biggest Sensation in California since the Discovery of Gold in 1849?" he asked in one advertisement. "WHY! HARRY HOUDINI! The ONLY recognized and Undisputed King of Handcuffs and Monarch of Leg Shackles."

The business cards he quickly had printed declared that he was the "only Conjurer in the World that Escapes out of all Handcuffs, Leg Shackles, Insane Belts and Strait Jackets after being STRIPPED STARK NAKED . . ."

Harry asked for and received a salary increase from Beck to one hundred twenty-five dollars a week. Within a year of signing with the German manager, he was receiving the then-astronomical sum of four hundred dollars a week, more than many American families earned in a year.

Not all was smooth sailing for the self-proclaimed

great escapist, however. In Kansas City, a practical joker locked him in a telephone booth and Houdini could not get out until someone brought the key. Reporters found out about the incident and Harry was afraid he would become the laughingstock of the country.

From then on he carried a pocketknifelike device containing steel picks that could open most locks.

Beck persuaded the Keith chain to sign Harry as a headliner on its eastern circuit, where he soon added to his growing reputation. In January 1900 in Boston, he met Capt. Charles Bean, inventor of the Bean Giant handcuffs. Bean cuffs were made of sheets of steel that held the wrists so rigidly they could not move toward each other. They were used in penitentiaries and jails throughout the country. Bean offered five hundred dollars to anyone who could open the cuffs, even if he gave them the key.

Bean knew that the cuffs were too far apart for anyone to reach the locks with the key. Unknown to him, however, Harry had designed a special extension rod that fit into the key and allowed him to easily reach the locks.

According to a reporter, Harry let the captain cuff his hands behind his back, then escaped from the Bean Giants.

"Well! Well!" Bean reportedly said. "I couldn't believe it unless it took place before my eyes. I have probably fastened ten thousand prisoners in my time with those handcuffs, and have met with all sorts of experiences, but — you beat me."

Harry's ego apparently kept pace with his steadily growing reputation. He complained about the percentage he had to pay Beck, and demanded that the manager ask higher salaries for him.

"I do not want instructions from you," Beck finally told him. "I am fully capable to know what to do. It is of no use for you to get the swelled head, as we are cutting heads off every day."

Houdini continued to complain about his contract, however, and sometimes deliberately made Beck wait for his percentage.

"At the time I made the contract . . . nobody knew that you are on earth," an angry Beck wrote him, "and it was only through my prestige and influence that you received these dates, which you seem to have forgotten so very soon."

But Harry was more convinced than ever of his greatness, and now advertised his act as "one of the greatest magical feats since biblical times."

He also began to make up stories about his background, a practice he would continue for the rest of his life. One reporter, after being told Houdini was from Europe, marveled that he spoke English so well, though he "learned it no one knows where."

Reporters were also impressed by his physique. Part of Harry's ability to successfully perform his escapes depended on raw physical strength, and he worked hard at developing that strength. Though short, reporters compared his muscular development favorably to that of the most renowned bodybuilder of his time, Eugene Sandow. One reporter described Harry's forearm as "a pillar of steel."

Harry did all he could to further that view by sending out hundreds of photos of himself clad only in a loincoth, standing by a jail cell ready to perform the "Naked Test."

His eastern tour continued to go well until he appeared at the New York Theater in Manhattan.

"The path of the handcuff king is not always roses," Harry had told a reporter in San Francisco, and now the truth of that statement was brought home to him.

He and Bess were still closing the act with Metamorphosis, and it had always gone smoothly. But that suddenly changed at the end of their first performance at the New York Theater. After Bess made the substitution for him by crawling inside the trunk, Harry pulled back the curtains for the audience, unwound the rope fastened around the trunk, then knelt beside the locks to open them.

To his chagrin, however, he found that he had left the keys to the locks in the fifth-floor dressing room. People who hurried to the room came back and said they couldn't find them.

While the audience roared with laughter, Bess was pounding on the trunk from inside, yelling, "Let me out! Let me out!" Someone finally found the keys, and Harry opened the trunk, only to find that she had fainted and he had to lift her out.

When Bess regained consciousness, she was not in a good mood. From then on she made sure the stage manager carried a second set of keys to open the trunk.

Far from it being the humiliation Harry feared, however, the incident resulted in publicity that packed the theater for the rest of their engagement.

After the Keith tour ended in February, Harry fulfilled a few more engagements he had contracted for. In April he escaped from the Kansas City jail after being bound by five pairs of leg and wrist irons and locked in a cell.

The lock on the cell was "guaranteed by the makers to be burglar-proof," the police declared, but Harry was out in just under eight minutes.

He was now twenty-six. He and Bess had just enjoyed their first year of success, and the Orpheum-Keith circuits would have been happy to have them back the next season. But Harry had other plans.

They were going to Europe, he told Bess. There was no guarantee they would succeed, they knew no one there, and they had saved only enough money for their passage and a few days' living expenses once they arrived. But it was the kind of gamble Harry would take throughout his life, a gamble he felt he had to take to become as famous as he was determined to be.

They sailed for England aboard the SS *Kensington* on May 30, 1900. During his years of struggling he had been billed as "the Great Wizard," a "European illusionist," "Projea, the Wild Man of Mexico," "Mysterious Harry Houdini," "Houdini the Great," and "The Genius of Escape," among other titles.

When he sailed for Europe, however, it was as "Harry Houdini, the King of Handcuffs."

Except for two brief visits, he would not return

to the United States for almost five years. When he did come back, he would be the biggest star in international vaudeville: A man known throughout the world simply as "Houdini."

His decision to go to Europe was destined to be the greatest and most successful gamble of his life.

four

Houdini and Bess settled in a rooming house in London while he made the rounds of theatrical agents. To his surprise, however, none of them were impressed by his exploits or his press clippings.

Finally he met a young man named Harry Day, who succeeded in getting him a one-week engagement at the Alhambra Theatre. There were five hundred vaudeville houses in or near London, and the Alhambra was one of the best. It seated 1,800 people and had standing room for another 2,200.

Houdini's routine included card tricks and Metamorphosis, but the escapes were the heart of his act.

At a special press performance prior to opening night, a man who billed himself as "Cirnoc, the Original King of Handcuffs," ran down the aisle shouting that Houdini was a fake.

Quick as always to see an opportunity for publicity, Houdini whispered to Bess to bring out the Bean Giant handcuffs. He then challenged Cirnoc to put them on, but Cirnoc refused.

Houdini put the cuffs on himself and stepped behind a screen. Using his hidden extension rod to open the locks, he emerged almost immediately with the cuffs hanging open.

Cirnoc then allowed himself to be cuffed with the Bean Giants and Houdini even gave him the key, knowing there was no way he could reach the locks without the extension rod.

Cirnoc struggled desperately for several minutes as he tried in vain to free himself. When he finally admitted defeat and asked Houdini to free him, the audience roared.

The publicity from the incident helped draw crowds to the Alhambra all week. The manager then offered to extend Houdini's performance if he could escape from handcuffs put on him by members of Scotland Yard, the London police department's famous detective division.

This was just what Houdini wanted and he seized the opportunity. Before coming to England he had studied British handcuffs and knew there were only seven or eight different makes. He knew that the most popular ones, called "English Regulation" cuffs, could be opened simply by rapping them in the right place against a hard object.

He had also found time during his few days in London to visit locksmith shops, and received permission to take apart several locks to see how they worked.

In the months to come, Houdini even developed a master key that could open all the different styles of regulation handcuffs used in the British Isles. (During his career, Houdini would study the drawings of every lock patented in the United States, Great Britain, and Germany).

The Alhambra manager took him to the office of Scotland Yard's superintendent, a man named Melville. Superintendent Melville handcuffed him to a pillar in the corridor, telling the manager he'd let "the American lad" stay there while they went back to the office.

"If you're going back to the office," Houdini reportedly said as they started to walk away, "I'll go with you."

Startled, Melville turned around to see Houdini standing to one side of the pillar and smiling broadly. The opened handcuffs lay on the floor.

The manager quickly signed Houdini for another

two weeks at the Alhambra, where Houdini performed before capacity crowds for a run that eventually totaled six months.

London newspapers were filled with stories about the "marvelous gentleman who frees himself in marvelously quick fashion of fetters, manacles, and all sorts of frightful things."

Houdini soon became even more popular in England than he had been in the United States. It was not just the tricks themselves that fascinated his audiences, but the tremendous flair and showmanship with which he did them.

Houdini used "Pomp and Circumstance" as his entrance music throughout most of his career, and one man said "he would allow many bars of that to go by after his name was spoken, before he would burst upon the stage . . . And he'd smile from ear to ear, and the audience would eat it up and break out in applause."

The public in London was awed by his challenge escapes, as he dared audience members to bind him with their own handcuffs, leg irons, and even straitjackets. Though few of them took him up on his challenges, they were thrilled by his ability to defeat anyone who did.

In a "£1,000 Challenge Open to the World," he

declared, "I, HARRY HOUDINI, known as the King of Handcuffs, at last becoming tired of so-called FAKE EXPOSURES AND MEDIOCRE MAGICIANS, who claim to DO MY ACT because they possess a lot of false keys and springs, DO HEREBY CHALLENGE any person in the world to duplicate my release from cuffs, irons, and straitjackets . . ."

One detective brought a pair of cuffs he said had been specially made to foil Houdini, and offered to be £50 ($250) he could not get out of them. Surprised when Houdini accepted the offer, the embarrassed detective admitted he didn't have £50. But after examining the cuffs to make sure they worked, Houdini allowed them to be snapped onto his wrists anyway.

He then "released himself from the new cuffs in ridiculously easy fashion," reported a theatrical publication called *The Music Hall*.

After his engagement at the Alhambra, Houdini toured the English provinces, then traveled to Dresden, Germany, in the fall of 1900. While waiting backstage on opening night at the Central Theater, the manager told him he would be fired if he wasn't an immediate hit.

"You can well imagine my feelings," Houdini wrote. "This manager had brought me to the continent with a contract which enabled him to close me right after my first performance if I was not a success, and I was not aware of that fact until just before going on. I was in no mood to do very much talking . . . I had never addressed an audience in German before. I must have said some of the most awful things to make them believe I was good."

The idea that a man could defy the authorities by breaking out of their harshest restraints was popular in all countries, but especially in Germany. The German police controlled all aspects of the people's lives, from the sale of food to the inspection of rooming houses. They also made sure that no entertainers criticized the government. As a result, Houdini's act, like that of all other performers, had to be approved by them.

"Every singer and vaudeville comedian must submit his entire act, in typewritten form, to the police fourteen days before date of opening," Houdini said. "The police look the matter over, and if there is anything about it that they don't like, such material is promptly cut out."

Audience members went wild at the conclusion of Houdini's first act at the Dresden theater, an escape from heavy prison handcuffs. He later described their reaction with his usual enthusiasm for his own accomplishments.

"When that audience rose in a solid mass . . . ," he said, "I knew I was going to stay my full engagement. And above all the din and noise and shouts and screams of the public, I heard Herr Direktor Kammsetzer's voice shouting like a madman. He ran to the middle of the stage and applauded. He took off his hat and he cheered. In fact, I have no fear of saying that I recorded with him the greatest triumph of any artiste he had ever engaged."

Houdini not only escaped from handcuffs that first night, but also from leg irons and manacles brought from a German prison. Some of the locks he opened weighed forty pounds.

Audiences packed the theater for the rest of his engagement, and theater managers throughout Germany outbid one another in their attempts to hire him. The police continued to be suspicious of him, however.

In Berlin, he had to strip naked before a crowd of three hundred policemen. The head of the Berlin police then supervised while policemen locked his arms behind his back with thumbscrews and five different kinds of elbow and hand irons.

Houdini was allowed to work beneath a blanket, and freed himself in six minutes. The police grudgingly acknowledged his achievement, but Houdini never trusted them. They walked around with long swords, he said, and "looked fierce as if hunting for trouble."

German newspapers were also slow to accept him, probably in part because of the widespread anti-American feeling in Germany and partly because he was a Jew. Houdini claimed he had never encountered anti-Semitism in the United States, but he had no trouble finding it in Germany.

The German audiences were as enthusiastic as any he had played before, however. In the industrial city of Essen, the managers of the massive Krupp armament factory (which would supply the German armed forces with weapons in World War I and World War II) bought out the theater for a special performance by him. They even designed handcuffs and leg irons they thought were escape-proof. Workers from Krupp locked them on him, then padlocked an iron collar around his neck. Then they chained his legs and arms together so tightly that he was pulled into a squatting position and couldn't even walk.

The men carried him into his cabinet, closed the

curtains, and waited confidently for Houdini to admit defeat. The orchestra played as the minutes ticked by and the audience became more and more anxious. Suddenly, after eleven minutes, Houdini emerged from the cabinet. He was disheveled but free.

The largest audience in the theater's history cheered so loudly the building seemed to shake.

"Not [alone] was the theater sold out, but hundreds were turned away," reported the local newspaper. "Contrary to fire and police regulations, the aisles were packed and even the scenery had been removed and chairs were placed on the stage to accommodate the public. Not even the fearful heat could keep away this sweltering mass of humanity and prevent it from giving Houdini an ovation."

Not only was he given an ovation, but the manager of the theater presented him with a massive three-foot-tall silver trophy surmounted by an eagle with wings outspread. Houdini was so moved that the speech he gave brought the audience to its feet.

He was now in demand throughout Europe. His successes in Germany were followed by a return engagement at the Alhambra in London and in the English provinces, then back to Germany again.

His act brought such a demand for escape artists

that he wired his brother Theo to join him, saying, "Come over, the apples are ripe." Theo wasted no time in crossing the Atlantic and performed as "Hardeen" for the rest of his life.

While Theo did many of the same tricks as well as his brother, the effect was not the same. "It seems to be the prevailing impression," a friend wrote Houdini, "that while he does the Handcuffs etc. etc. apparently as good as Houdini <u>He does not make it go</u> with the audience or in other words — he is not the <u>showman</u> Houdini is."

Houdini's success brought many imitators, but perhaps the one who infuriated him most was his old friend from the necktie firm, Jacob Hyman. Hyman, who had suggested that young Ehrich Weiss use the name "Houdini" and performed briefly with him as half of the "Brothers Houdini," was performing in the United States as "The Great Houdini, King of Handcuffs."

Hyman claimed he had as much legal right to use the name as his onetime friend. "Perhaps he has," Houdini replied, "but he has no honor."

Houdini bragged that he had now become so famous that "in Berlin, when someone meets you and tenders you some news, instead of saying

'Is that so?' the exclamation of the listener is 'Ha-Houdini!'"

Throughout his life, Houdini deeply missed his mother whenever they were separated. On his tour through Europe, he saved every letter she wrote and constantly thought of ways to make her happy.

"No one in the world could have a better mother than I do," he told a German reporter, "and my mother is the dearest person on earth to me."

It had been nine years since he had promised his dying father to take care of his mother. Houdini had faithfully kept that promise, sending her money even when he had little for himself and Bess, but now he wanted to do something special for her.

In the summer of 1901 he brought her to Germany and gave her a gown that had reportedly been made for England's Queen Victoria. According to the story, the queen died before the gown was finished and it was put up for sale in a London shop. Houdini bought it and Bess did the alterations so it would fit Cecilia Weiss.

Mrs. Weiss arrived in Hamburg and attended a sold-out performance by her son, sitting in a chair he had placed in a box overlooking the stage. It would be hard to say who was prouder as she watched him perform, mother or son.

The next day, continuing the honor he was determined to bring his mother, Houdini took her and Bess by train to Budapest, Hungary. Cecilia had left Hungary as the frightened young wife of a man who would always struggle in poverty, but now she was returning as the mother of a man whose name was known throughout Europe.

Houdini arranged for a reception for her in the fanciest hotel in Budapest. His mother, dressed in Queen Victoria's gown and seated by her son in a gilded chair as if on a throne, greeted friends and relatives she had not seen for more than a quarter of a century.

"How my heart warmed to see the various friends and relatives kneel and pay homage to Mother, every inch a Queen . . . ," Houdini said. "Mother and I were awake all night talking over the affair, and if happiness ever entered my life to its fullest, it was sharing Mother's wonderful enjoyment at playing a queen for a day. The next morning, after having lived two ecstatically happy days, I escorted the Fairy Queen en route to America."

It was, Houdini said many years later, the happiest day of his life.

Houdini's father, Rabbi Mayer Weiss *(Houdini Historical Center, Outgamie County Historical Society, Appleton, WI)*

Houdini's first magic tricks book, with hand-written notes by Houdini *(Harry Ransom Humanities Research Center, University of Texas, Austin)*

Houdini (Erich Weiss) as a youth pictured with track medals. His physical dexterity would prove him capable of enduring dangerous feats. *(Library of Congress)*

Harry and Bess Houdini (at far right in front row) with the
Welsh Brothers Circus in 1895 *(Library of Congress)*

Houdini (pictured center) with his brothers (from left to
right) Leopold, Hardeen, Bill and Nat *(Library of Congress)*

The young couple, Bess and Houdini, in their first year of marriage, as "America's Greatest Comedy Act" *(Library of Congress)*

Houdini with his wife, Bess, and his mother, Cecilia Steiner Weiss, 1907 *(Library of Congress)*

Rochester N.Y. 1908

Houdini with his much-loved mother in Rochester, New York *(Library of Congress)*

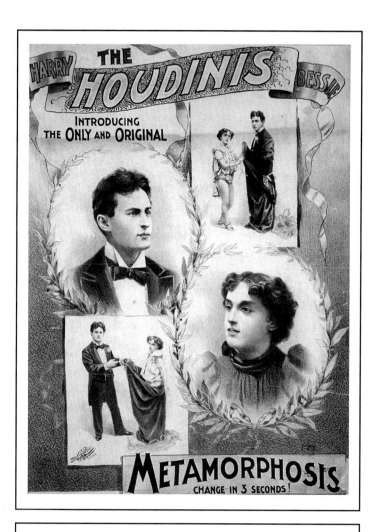

One of Houdini and Bess's posters that generated interest in their traveling shows *(Library of Congress)*

The charming Houdini and Bess five years after their marriage *(Library of Congress)*

five

Houdini was now so busy that he hired an assistant, a former officer in the Austrian army named Franz Kukol. Kukol helped him during his performances, arranged for demonstrations at police stations, and contacted newspaper reporters for the publicity Houdini stirred up in every town.

The German police continued to be suspicious of Houdini, but Kukol persuaded officials in one city to let him try a new trick: jumping into the river while bound with handcuffs, leg irons, and chains.

Underwater escapes while chained and handcuffed were especially dangerous, and Houdini said they required "extreme carefulness."

They also required the performer to have tremendous courage and the ability to hold his breath for a long time. Houdini worked hard at increasing his lung capacity by running, swimming underwater, and holding his breath while submerged in a tub filled with water.

As for courage, he always had it. He once said that his chief task throughout his career had been "to conquer fear. When I am stripped and manacled, nailed securely within a weighted packing case and thrown into the sea, or when I am buried alive under six feet of earth, it is necessary to preserve absolute serenity of spirit. . . . If I grow panicky I am lost."

Somehow he managed to preserve his serenity of spirit and not to panic, no matter how difficult the escape.

His jump into the German river set the pattern for those that would follow. He stayed underwater so long the spectators were afraid he had drowned, but then he bobbed up, smiling triumphantly, and holding the chains aloft.

The crowd roared its approval, but when he walked ashore the police arrested him for walking on the grass.

Houdini had been using his spare money to buy books and other items for his budding library, which would eventually become the largest magic library in the United States. He also had a great respect for elderly magicians and often sought them out, eagerly listening to their experiences.

One of these magicians was Alexander Heimberger, who was now eighty-four years old. As a young man with a stage name of Alexander the Conjurer, he had been the first magician to perform at the White House and was even mentioned in Herman Melville's novel, *Moby-Dick*.

Seeing all the materials about magic that Heimberger showed him, Houdini said, "was like having the history of magic unrolled before my eager eyes."

He also bought letters, programs, and any other items he could find about his boyhood hero, Robert-Houdin. When his travels finally took him to Paris at the end of 1901, he sent a telegram to Robert-Houdin's daughter-in-law.

"With all the respect due you in the world, and as a great admirer of the justly celebrated and famous conjurer Robert-Houdin," he wrote, "I . . . ask your consent to permit me, as a representative of American Magicians, to place a wreath on the tomb of Robert-Houdin . . ."

She rejected his request, saying she was ill, and also refused to meet with him. Houdini traveled to the cemetery anyway and placed a huge wreath on the grave. On the wreath were the words, "Honor and respect to Robert-Houdin from the Magicians of America."

He took a photographer along to record the moment, as he would for the rest of his life when he placed wreaths on the graves of magicians.

Then he stood "for fully half an hour . . . with my hat in my [sic] at the tomb of Robert-Houdin, and with all the reverence and homage with which I respect his memory."

Houdini never forgave an insult, and many people have speculated that the refusal of Robert-Houdin's daughter-in-law to see him stirred an anger that lasted the rest of his life. This may explain why, seven years later, he wrote a book called *The Unmasking of Robert-Houdin*, in which he called his childhood hero "a mere pretender, a man who waxed great on the brainwork of others."

Houdini interrupted his European performances to make a quick business trip to the United States in the spring of 1902. One of the people he met was Martin Beck, who advised him to stay in Europe and continue to take advantage of his popularity there.

When Houdini returned to Germany, he was more famous than ever because of a lawsuit he had won against a German policeman named Werner

Graff. Graff had said in a newspaper that Houdini's claim that he could escape from any police restraint was false, and that he had tried to bribe the police and arrange a phony escape from the Cologne jail. Houdini sued him for slander.

Graff brought a special lock to court, which the judge ordered Houdini to prove he could open without using a key. Houdini opened the lock by banging it against a metal plate on his leg until it weakened.

He was then chained and locked, and ordered to release himself. The judge allowed him to go to a corner, where only the judge could see what he did. Houdini easily freed himself, but was furious he had to do it with the judge watching.

"Just imagine," he told a friend. "In order to save my honor I had to show how I did it."

The court ordered Graff and the newspaper to pay a small fine, and the newspaper printed an apology. The outcome resulted in a publicity bonanza for Houdini, who milked it for all it was worth.

OFFICIAL POLICE NEWS FROM GERMANY! a flier he had printed read. HARRY HOUDINI THE AMERICAN HANDCUFF KING SUES THE COLOGNE POLICE FOR LIBEL AND WINS.

His victory, he declared, was "the greatest feat I

ever accomplished." The German people "fear the police so much, in fact the Police are all Mighty and I am the first man that has ever dared them."

Whatever country he was performing in, Houdini liked to speak the native language, saying "it makes them all friendly with me, before I have performed a single trick."

This usually worked well, even though one reviewer described his German as "a droll gibberish of American English and Berlin German." But when he performed in Copenhagen, Denmark, his broken Danish was so bad the audience mistook him for a comedian and roared with laughter.

The more successful Houdini became, the more imitators and challengers he encountered. He treated them all like he treated anyone who made him angry: by trying to destroy their reputations and humiliating them.

A German magician calling himself "Hilmar the Uncuffable" made the mistake of challenging Houdini before a packed crowd of four thousand people in Berlin's Wintergarten.

Striding onto the stage, Hilmar bragged he could perform escapes no American could match. Houdini quickly snapped a pair of handcuffs on him that required two keys to open, and dared him to escape.

After several minutes in Houdini's cabinet, Hilmar emerged "still cuffed and 'red as a lobster.'" Houdini hauled him down to the footlights and demanded that he admit he couldn't get out of the cuffs. When Hilmar refused, Houdini told him to go find a locksmith, because he was not going to release him.

"He then showed his cur spirit and cried like a spanked babe," Houdini said. "He cringed and fawned like a dog and begged me to unlock him. I refused, but he cried so much the audience felt sorry and cried out, 'He is beaten enough. Please release him.'"

Houdini finally uncuffed Hilmar the Uncuffable, but continued to be furious at him, calling the German magician "Mr. Slob E. Hiller . . . who cleans the spittoons, washes windows, and runs errands for a cigar store."

Houdini's fame brought him an invitation to perform in Russia in the spring of 1903, and he accepted. Russia was ruled by Czar Nicholas II, and his police controlled every aspect of Russian life.

The chief of police in Moscow exercised so much power, Houdini discovered, that "should he take a dislike to you he can compel you to leave Moscow inside of twenty-four hours, and there will be no questions asked."

And while Houdini had encountered anti-Semitism in Germany, it was nothing compared to the hatred against Jews he found in Russia. Jews were not allowed to enter the country and theater managers were not permitted to hire Jewish performers.

Houdini's arrival in Russia coincided with a two-day orgy of murder, torture, and looting against Jews in Bessarabia, a city of approximately 150,000. He visited the scene and declared that "nothing like it could occur in any country but Russia."

It is surprising that Houdini was allowed to enter Russia since Jewish visitors were banned. But Houdini reportedly listed his religion as "Catholic" on his passport. Despite feeling uncomfortable his entire time there, Houdini was a great success and was even invited to perform before the nobility. One of his performances was for the Grand Duke Sergei Aleksandrovich, the governor-general of Moscow. One of the first acts of the Grand Duke when he was appointed twelve years before, had been to expel twenty thousand Jews from Moscow.

Houdini gave a private performance for the Grand Duke, who rewarded him with an ornamental champagne ladle. Houdini proudly estimated the ladle was worth more than five hundred dollars. He apparently never said publicly why he agreed to perform before a man who had persecuted Jews or what he felt about it.

Houdini had his first encounter with the Russian police shortly after he arrived. He was determined to present his performances in Russian, even though he knew almost nothing about the language.

In order to practice in a large setting, he went to what he thought was an empty racetrack and bellowed such lines as "I challenge any police official to handcuff me," and "I defy the police departments of the world to hold me."

He had felt all along that "spy detectives" were watching his movements, and he quickly found out he was right. Within minutes, the police surrounded him and carried him off. Bess was finally able to talk them into releasing him.

Houdini had seen the infamous convict caravans that were a regular feature of life under the czar. Criminals and those who opposed the czar were marched through the streets on their way to Siberia.

Each caravan contained what was called a Siberian wagon, which Houdini said looked "very like a large safe on wheels."

These horse-drawn jail cells had walls made of solid steel lined with sheets of zinc, with a single padlocked door in the back. The only opening in the door was a tiny window covered by iron bars. The lock to the door was about thirty inches below the window. There were no sanitary facilities in the wagons, and convicts locked inside were kept there for the entire journey to Siberia.

In addition, the door could only be unlocked by a different key than the one that locked it: a key in the possession of a prison official on the Siberian border, about a twenty-one-day journey from Moscow.

Houdini convinced the head of Moscow's secret police to let him try to break out of a Siberian wagon. The chief remained suspicious of him and insisted there be no publicity. He also forced Houdini to submit to a surprise strip search by prison doctors, who made him take off all his clothes. They then probed every part of his body, from the soles of his feet to the top of his head, but found no hidden tools or keys on him.

Still naked, he was locked in the wagon after being shackled with iron bands around his wrists and ankles. The chief granted Houdini's request to back the wagon against a wall so the police could not see him work on the lock.

The police laughed as they listened to Houdini's struggles in the wagon, confident he would fail. In about forty-five minutes, however (which he later claimed was "less than twelve"), Houdini swung open the door in triumph and walked out.

The smile on his face quickly vanished when the furious police grabbed him and made him undergo another strip search. They also stripped and searched Franz Kukol, who was with him, but found nothing on either one. Bess was also there, but they did not search her.

Houdini never explained how he managed to escape from the supposedly escape-proof wagon. Bess or Kukol may have been able to slip him the necessary tools or even a duplicate key to the door, but that would have been extremely difficult and dangerous. And even if he had the key, he would still have needed a long extension device to reach the keyhole.

However he managed to pull off the feat, the chief refused to give him the certificate he had promised if the escape was successful. Word of Houdini's triumph somehow spread throughout

Russia anyway, undoubtedly aided by Houdini. It was, he claimed with his usual enthusiasm for his accomplishments, "the biggest sensation that has ever been up here."

He performed in Russia for five months, earning more than he had ever earned before. But he and Bess both breathed sighs of relief when they finally left, "thankful to think that nothing had happened to transport us to Siberia."

After leaving Russia, they traveled to Holland and Germany, where Houdini's amazing success continued.

"The sun shines for me every day," he wrote a friend. But even in the midst of his triumphs and huge salaries, he remained haunted by the poverty of his childhood. He sent money home for the rainy days he was sure were coming, and traveled in third-class railroad cars because they were the cheapest ones available.

Never "have I forgotten the fact that 'life is but an empty dream,'" he said.

His determination to stay at the top of his profession led to escapes that were increasingly daring. One of the most spectacular occurred at the London Hippodrome theater on March 17, 1904.

Five days earlier, a reporter from the *London Daily Illustrated Mirror* had stepped onstage and challenged Houdini to open a pair of handcuffs that had taken five years to make.

The blacksmith who made them claimed it had taken him a week just to fashion the key, and that not even he could pick the lock. London's finest locksmiths agreed that "they had never before seen such wonderful mechanism."

The lock was patterned after one invented in the eighteenth century, which was used to guard the state secrets of England. Despite a large reward for anyone who could open it, no one could do so for sixty-one years. Finally a famous lock-picker succeeded, but it took him forty-four hours.

Houdini accepted the *Mirror*'s challenge, and the massive publicity that followed put "London in an uproar," he declared.

Four thousand spectators and more than one hundred reporters packed the Hippodrome on the afternoon of the attempt. When Houdini stepped onstage, the *Mirror* reported, he "received an ovation worthy of a monarch, one of the finest ovations mortal man has ever received."

A committee of several dozen volunteers was

called to the stage to make sure Houdini received no help.

The handcuffs were riveted to a long piece of steel that looked like a sawed-off shotgun. Frank Smith, a reporter from the *Mirror*, snapped them over Houdini's wrists, then slowly turned the key six times while the bolt slammed firmly into place.

Houdini then retired to his cabinet (which he called his "ghost house") and closed its red curtains. The audience waited anxiously while the orchestra played and Houdini struggled out of their sight. Once he stuck his head out so he could examine the lock under the strong stage lights.

After thirty-five minutes he emerged a second time.

"His [shirt] collar was broken," reported the *Mirror*, "water trickled in great channels down his face, and he looked generally warm and uncomfortable."

Houdini said his knees hurt, and Smith agreed to give him a cushion to kneel on. Twenty minutes later, Houdini emerged again. He was still handcuffed and asked that they be taken off so he could remove his coat.

When Smith refused, Houdini responded with the showmanship, defiance, and courage that seemed to come as naturally to him as breathing. He managed to remove a pen knife from his jacket pocket and open it with his teeth, turn his coat inside out over his head, then slash it to pieces with the knife while the audience "yelled themselves frantic."

Houdini reentered the cabinet, where he struggled for another ten minutes while the orchestra played a "stirring march." Suddenly, "with a great shout of victory," he bounded through the curtains, holding the opened cuffs in his hands. It had been one hour and ten minutes since he first entered the cabinet.

"A mighty roar of gladness went up," the *Mirror* reported. "Men waved their hats, shook hands one with the other. Ladies waved their handkerchiefs, and the committee, rushing forward as one man, shouldered Houdini, and bore him in triumph around the arena."

To this day, no one is sure how Houdini managed to free himself. There has been speculation that Bess passed him the key in a glass of water. But the key was large, the water clear, and Frank Smith carefully examined every object Houdini handled.

No matter how he accomplished the feat, it was headlined in papers throughout England, and theaters competed to sign him up. The years of strain were beginning to wear him down, though. A few weeks later, for the first time in his career, he canceled a date because of illness.

Four years earlier he had told a doctor that his nerves "are all run down and I am not well as the prepetual [sic] worry and excitement is beginning to tell on me and I am afraid that if I don't take a rest soon I'll be all done up."

Although he was only thirty-one years old, Houdini had been performing his physically demanding act professionally for thirteen years. He now began to talk of retiring. He and Bess sailed to the United States for a vacation in April 1904, and spent the summer there.

He took his mother for long walks, bought her hot chocolate at the drugstore, and even went shopping with her.

He and Theo made a sentimental journey to Appleton, where they visited several old friends of the family. Houdini gave them gifts of money, and bought new clothes for two old men.

When he returned to New York City, he went to see the tenement the family had lived in when his father was still alive.

Although Houdini lived in an era of blatant anti-black discrimination, he had always seemed untouched by it. In England he had noted with approval that there were many popular black performers, and that they were treated as well as white ones.

"Were I a colored man," he wrote, "I would never leave this country."

But after visiting the tenement where he and his family had lived in poverty for so many years, he wrote in his diary, "I'd hate to live there now." Then he made derogatory comments on the African-Americans and Cubans living there.

In his views about race, as in so many other areas of his life, there seemed to be two Houdinis struggling with each other.

Despite his success, he and Bess had never owned a house. One of the first things he did after arriving in the United States was to buy a four-story brownstone in Harlem. It had twenty-six rooms, including twelve bedrooms, as well as several baths and fireplaces.

Harlem boasted one of the largest populations of eastern European Jews in the country, and living there was considered a sure sign of financial success. Houdini moved his mother into the house, along with his sister Gladys, brothers William and Leopold, and a young German servant named Anna Aulbach.

Another part of his dream had come true. The Harlem brownstone would be his mother's home for the rest of her life, and the place he would always return to in the years to come.

six

The house was important to Houdini both as a symbol of his success and as yet another way of fulfilling his promise to take care of his mother.

But it was also important for another reason: It gave him the space he needed to hold his growing collection of books and memorabilia on magic. Although he had gained the world's respect as a performer, Houdini wanted desperately to be respected as an educated man who knew the value of books and writing.

"We have records for five generations," he said, "that my direct forefathers were students and teachers of the Bible and recognized as among the leading bibliographers of their times."

He bragged that his father had left him all his books, and declared that his father was his favorite author. Between performances and on his days off, Houdini roamed bookstores in England, France,

Germany, and the United States, looking for rare, secondhand books on magic.

Eventually he expanded his collection beyond the field of magic. He was a great admirer of Abraham Lincoln, and accumulated the largest number of Lincoln letters of any private collector. He also tracked down the original signatures or letters of almost all the signers of the Declaration of Independence; bought the original Martin Luther Bible, with notes in the margins written by Luther; and even purchased a writing desk used by the poet and short-story writer, Edgar Allan Poe.

"If his attention had early been turned in the direction of scholarship," said one friend, "he would have achieved fame as a scholar."

One of the most memorable experiences of Houdini's life occurred in 1904 when a former magician named Henry Evans Evanion sought him out. Houdini was staying at a London hotel at the time, when the frail-looking 72-year-old man approached him in the lobby.

Evanion, whom Houdini later described as the "absolute greatest collector of magicians' material that ever lived," had come to show Houdini a few of the rare playbills, programs, advertisements, and lithographs of magicians from his large collection.

Houdini was amazed to see original programs of Robert-Houdin and other famous magicians that he had thought were lost forever.

"I remember raising my hands before my eyes, as if I had been dazzled by a sudden shower of diamonds . . . ," he said. "I felt as if the King of England stood before me and I must do him homage."

In the months to come, Houdini bought many items from Evanion, and the grateful man gave him many others.

"I treated the old man as if he had been my father," Houdini said. The two became fast friends and when Evanion died a little over a year later, Houdini advertised the funeral in the newspapers and paid all expenses. Later, when Evanion's widow died, he paid for her funeral, too.

Now, with his purchase of the house in Harlem, Houdini had room to begin arranging his collection. He and Bess also talked about having children.

"[My] wife says she wishes she could raise children and stop working," he said, "and perhaps in 1905 we may rest long enough to raise one of them things called children ourselves."

The couple would remain childless the rest of their lives, however, a fact that always pained them.

At the end of the summer, Houdini returned to England. Crowds again packed the theaters, and he spent a year breaking records wherever he performed. In one theater, where he arranged for a percentage of the receipts instead of a straight salary, he cleared $2,150 in one week.

Houdini's final performance before returning to the United States was at a theater in Leith, Scotland, on July 8, 1904. He told the audience it had been five years since he had performed in America, and now he was going home.

The crowd leaped to their feet, cheering and shouting. When he left the theater, several men hoisted him on their shoulders and carried him to the railroad station while spectators sang, "And when ye go, will ye nae come back?"

Houdini was so moved by this outpouring of affection, he said, that he "wept like a child."

Back in the United States, he prepared himself for stunts more daring than any he had attempted before. He was driven both by his inner need for perfection and by the need to stay ahead of his many imitators.

The new tricks would involve holding his breath underwater or escaping from dark, confined spaces. To gain the lung capacity the tricks required, Houdini installed a large sunken tub in the house, where he practiced holding his breath underwater.

Sometimes he practiced in water at normal temperatures and sometimes in icy water that was near freezing. He also built up his lung capacity by running and swimming long distances.

"If it had not been for my athletic boyhood," he once said in discussing the importance of his strength, "I would never have been Houdini."

Before introducing his new escapes, however, he repeated some of the old ones. In January 1906, in a brilliant move that brought him massive publicity throughout the United States, Houdini escaped from a cell in the federal prison in Washington, D.C.

The cell had once held Charles J. Guiteau, the assassin of President James A. Garfield, and was currently occupied by a man who had smothered his wife. It was in the middle of a row of cells walled in by solid brick, with a narrow, bulletproof oak door set three feet back from the corridor.

An iron bar on the door projected out to the corridor, and bent at a right angle to reach the lock on the corridor wall. The bar slipped over a steel catch, which set a spring and fastened a lock with five tumblers. All the locks were opened with the same key.

The cells contained two murderers waiting to be hanged, four accused murderers awaiting trial, a man convicted of manslaughter, and a burglar.

Houdini was stripped and searched, then locked into the cell. Somehow he freed himself within two minutes. But instead of calling the warden, he suddenly came up with an idea to make his escape even more spectacular.

Still nude, he opened all the other cells and made their startled occupants switch places, then locked them into their new cells.

"Have you come to let me out?" one hopeful inmate asked.

All the switching around took just twenty-one minutes. Houdini dressed, then strolled into the warden's office where the staff and several reporters waited.

"I let all of your prisoners out," he said as the warden's mouth flew open and a guard leaped toward the door. "But I locked them all in again."

His feat was covered by newspapers throughout the country, with the *Washington Post* reporting, "When the officials found what he had done with their prisoners, their amazement passed all bounds."

There was speculation that Houdini had managed to hide a key or his lock-picking tools in the cell. But even then it would have been extremely difficult for him to reach out to the corridor with some kind of extension, find the lock set back on the wall at a right angle, and fit the key into the lock.

I TOLD YOU SO!!! Houdini declared in an ad.

WHEN IT WAS DISCOVERED THAT HOUDINI, "THE PRISON DEFIER," HAD BEEN BROUGHT BACK TO AMERICA AT A SALARY OF $1,000 WEEKLY, ALL THE WISENHEIMERS AND SOCIETY OF KNOW-IT-ALL FELLOWS POLISHED UP THEIR HAMMERS, SAYING, "GOLD BRICK!"

IT HAS NOW BEEN POSITIVELY PROVEN BEYOND ANY CONTRADICTION THAT HOUDINI IS THE HARDEST WORKING ARTIST THAT HAS EVER TRODDEN THE VAUDEVILLE STAGE!!

HE IS WORTH MORE THAN THE SALARY HE IS BOOKED FOR!!!

A few weeks after his escape from the federal prison, Houdini made an equally spectacular escape from the Boston city jail.

One sensational escape followed another during his Boston engagements in 1906 and 1907. It was as if he had become his greatest rival and was constantly trying to outdo himself.

A few days after his Boston jail escape, he was chained and padlocked inside a Witch's Chair, a torturous device made to hold women accused of being witches in Massachusetts Colony. The upper part of it enclosed his body so he could barely move, then chains were wound around him and fastened to the cage with padlocks.

It took him almost an hour and a half, but an exhausted Houdini finally stepped out of the cage to the cheers of over three thousand people.

The following week, in trying an escape he had never done before, Houdini almost met with failure. He never attempted an escape unless he or an assistant had carefully examined it from every angle. In fact, as he perfected his jail escapes, he or one of his assistants usually managed to hide his picks and keys in or near the cell.

His main assistant was Franz Kukol, but he later hired two other men, Jim Collins and James Vickery, who stayed with them the rest of his life. Both were young Englishmen, extremely competent, and totally loyal to Houdini. He often fired them in temporary fits of anger, then became upset if they thought he meant it.

Houdini came up with the idea of allowing himself to be sealed in an iron boiler. It had been made by employees of the Riverside Boiler Works in nearby Cambridge, and was almost five feet high and two feet in diameter.

Houdini was chained and handcuffed, then placed into the boiler. Workmen clamped down the top and riveted in two long bolts to hold it down. Houdini then went to work in the pitch darkness inside, confident he would soon be out.

A boilermaker named Bert Clark stood next to Kukol in the wings, carefully watching the performance. Years later Clark revealed that Houdini had brought him to Boston to make a tiny pipe cutter and exact duplicates of the long bolts.

Houdini hid the cutter in his clothes, and took it out once he was inside the boiler. He planned to cut off the ends of the bolts, push them up, remove the top, and climb out. Then he would replace the top and fasten it down with the duplicate bolts, which he had hidden in the legs of his cabinet.

Neither Houdini, Clark, nor Kukol thought of the one problem that almost defeated him: As Houdini cut through the bolts, the slivers of metal that resulted stuck in the holes and prevented him from pushing the bolts up and out of the way.

Minutes passed as Houdini sweated in his cramped position in the blackness of the boiler.

Then finally he realized that if he took the cutter apart and used one piece as a hammer and the other piece as a spike, he could knock the bolts through the top.

The escape he had thought would take a few minutes took almost an hour. When he emerged from behind the curtain of his cabinet, wrote one reporter, he was "pale, weak, and trembling . . . hardly able to stand erect."

A headline in one of the Boston newspapers the next day read, "Houdini Victor in Supreme Test," and Houdini agreed. "This challenge is the limit," he wrote in his diary. "Greatest test I ever did."

During the next two years he escaped from every sort of restraint he or his challengers could devise. These included: a coffin with the lid screwed down and airholes for him to breathe through (fifty-eight minutes); a glass box bolted together with strips of steel fastened with two padlocks (thirty-six minutes); and a leather bag drawn tight by a heavy chain that was fastened with six locks (twenty-three minutes).

In addition to performing jail escapes in almost every town he visited, Houdini escaped from inside a giant leather football without disturbing the laces; several more boilers that were riveted shut; straitjackets; and various types of packing boxes, including one that had been left in the rain for two days so that all the boards were soaked and swollen.

In Toledo, Ohio, several teenage boys tied him up with thick ropes smeared with tar. It took Houdini forty-one minutes to finally free himself, and that night he wrote in his diary, "Hurt like hell."

Somehow Houdini also found time to publish the *Conjurers' Monthly Magazine*, a thirty-two-page periodical filled with his usual grammatical errors and misspellings. Houdini started the magazine after the editor of the *Sphinx*, which was published by the Society of American Magicians, refused to give him the free publicity he wanted.

Houdini used much of the space in his magazine to attack the *Sphinx*'s editor, Dr. A. M. Wilson, as well as his imitators and anyone else who had offended him. He even demanded that people choose between him and Dr. Wilson if they wanted to remain his friends.

When a fellow magician asked for a loan, Houdini replied, "I wrote you that a certain Dr. Wilson was a bitter enemy of mine. As you have seen fit to accept his friendship by writing for his paper . . . you can consider our years of friendship at an end and I trust you will have the good sense NEVER TO

WRITE ME OR APPROACH ME IN CASE I PLAY IN YOUR CITY."

Dr. Wilson responded to Houdini's criticism by writing, "I am sorry for him that money has become his god, and self-conceit has caused him to idolize himself."

Years after his angry attacks on Wilson, the two became as good friends as they had been bitter enemies. Houdini even gave Wilson a key to his house in Harlem so the doctor could stay there whenever he was in New York City.

But Houdini continued to react with anger whenever he felt slighted. In 1908, years after Robert-Houdin's daughter-in-law had refused to see him, he published *The Unmasking of Robert-Houdin*. Houdini challenged the public "to find one mis-representation . . . [or], in all the literature of magic, one book that can compare with mine."

Though few if any readers could have known it, there was one misrepresentation before the first chapter even began. Houdini dedicated the book to his father, "Rev. M. S. Weiss, Ph.D., LL.D.," giving him degrees and a title Mayer Weiss never earned.

Houdini used the book to try and destroy the reputation of the man who had once been his idol and was now seen as a competitor, even though he had been dead almost forty years. Robert-Houdin, he charged in the book, had "robbed dead-and-gone magicians of all credit for their inventions and accomplishments."

A few of Houdini's charges were true, but he seemed so driven to destroy his former hero that he ignored the Frenchman's many accomplishments.

From 1906 to 1908, Houdini successfully met every challenge thrown at him in first-class vaudeville houses throughout the United States. He also performed several spectacular jumps into rivers and canals while handcuffed or bound with chains. Ten thousand people crowded a levee at New Orleans to watch him jump into the Mississippi River. It was the first and last time he would try his escape from the deep, powerful currents of the country's mightiest river. His hands were cuffed behind his back, and a pair of irons was chained to the cuffs so tightly his elbows touched each other.

Another chain was wrapped across his chest and behind his back, where it was fastened to his wrists. Finally his chain was locked at the front of his throat.

Houdini leaped into the water from a small boat. After about half a minute his arm broke through the water, clutching the chains and locks, and then his head appeared.

The crowd roared its approval, but Houdini was shaken by the powerful currents of the river.

"That's an awful river," he said. "And the further down I went the colder and darker it became."

He also jumped into San Francisco Bay, a lake in Denver, the Charles River in Boston, the Atlantic Ocean from a pier in Atlantic City, and the Detroit River in Detroit.

For his jump into San Francisco Bay, Houdini had his hands cuffed behind his back and a seventy-five-pound iron ball chained to one ankle. He apparently never performed this dangerous feat again. If anything had gone wrong, the ball would have quickly dragged him to the bottom. There was no room for error underwater and he said the exploits were "dangerous business at the best."

One imitator drowned after being manacled and jumping into a river in Bavaria. Before Houdini's jump in Detroit, he was said to have handed Kukol a note which read, "I leave all to Bess."

As dangerous as these jumps were, Houdini felt his usual need to exaggerate.

His most famous jump was the one in Detroit, and years later he claimed it had been made through a hole chopped in the ice. He said he freed himself from the handcuffs, but was swept away from the hole by the current.

Unable to find the hole when he swam back, Houdini said he stayed alive by breathing air trapped in bubbles in the space just below the ice. After being trapped underwater for eight minutes, according to him, he finally found the hole and escaped.

Bess did her best to enlarge this tale. She claimed she was waiting for him in their hotel room when she heard newsboys calling out that Houdini was dead. Moments later, she said, he appeared at the door soaking wet and blue with cold.

It was a great story and one that Houdini added to throughout the years, but it is not true.

More than fifty years after the jump, a researcher found a front-page newspaper article in the *Detroit News* describing it: There was no ice in the river, Houdini had a safety rope tied around his waist all the time, he freed himself from the two pairs of police handcuffs on his wrists without any trouble, and he was quickly picked up by a waiting boat.

And obviously Bess did not hear newsboys announcing his death or see him appear at the door soaking wet and blue with cold.

Despite the massive publicity Houdini made sure he received from this and other jumps, however, the public was beginning to lose interest in the challenges and handcuff escapes.

"Manager Tate informs me, 'You are not worth a five-dollar bill to me,'" he wrote in his diary in St. Louis in January 1908. A few weeks later he wrote, "Arrived in Cleveland seven o'clock. Am not featured. Is this week the first step toward oblivion? No attention paid to me."

Houdini was determined not to descend into the oblivion he had feared since childhood, and which he had seen claim his father. Imitators had copied all his escapes, and he desperately wanted to develop one it would be almost impossible for them to copy.

He lay awake thinking up ideas and finally came up with one of the most impressive tricks he would ever perform: the Milk Can Escape. He practiced it for months before daring to try it onstage.

The escape involved a galvanized iron can the size and shape of the cans farmers used to deliver milk to dairies. It was just large enough for Houdini to squeeze into with his knees bent. Once the cover was in place, it was fastened down by at least six padlocks.

Water always added to the danger and difficulty

of Houdini's escapes, and this was especially true with the Milk Can Escape. His assistants poured twenty or more buckets of water into the can, then lowered him (dressed in a bathing suit) into the can feetfirst, with his wrists handcuffed.

When Houdini's head was submerged, the assistants clamped down the lid and locked it. Then they pulled the cabinet in place and closed the curtains.

"Ladies and gentlemen," Houdini said just before entering the can, "my latest invention . . . I will attempt to escape. Should anything happen, and should I fail to appear within a certain time, my assistants will open the curtains, rush in, smash the Milk Can and do everything possible to save my life. Music, Maestro, please."

While the orchestra slowly played "Asleep in the Deep" ("Many brave hearts lie asleep in the deep. Sailor, beware; sailor, take care"), Kukol stood by with a fire ax ready to smash open the can.

Some in the audience grew almost panic-stricken as time ticked by without any sign of Houdini: one minute, ninety seconds, two minutes, two and a half minutes, three minutes.

Kukol moved toward the can and raised his ax as several people yelled for him to smash the locks.

And then Houdini bounded through the curtains, soaking wet but smiling triumphantly. Behind him stood the can, with all its padlocks still closed and in place.

The audience went wild. It was a trick that would fascinate spectators for the rest of Houdini's life and one few imitators dared to try.

As impossible as it looked, the secret of the escape was simple: The rivets that seemed to hold the upper part of the can — the lid, neck, and shoulder — to the rest of the container were fake.

Once inside, all Houdini had to do after he slipped off the handcuffs was push up hard against the lid, and the entire upper part of the can came off. He then stepped out, replaced the lid, neck, and shoulder (with the padlocks still intact), and emerged from behind the curtain.

The simplicity of the Milk Can Escape was a stroke of genius, and the most careful examination of the can failed to reveal its secret.

Even with the escape's simplicity, it was still a dangerous stunt. It required the ability to perform quick movements while holding the breath for long periods in an uncomfortable, crouched position. All the movements also had to be made in pitch blackness, in a space so small it pressed against his sides and left no room for error.

Houdini's rare blend of strength, skill, and courage was what made it possible for him to perform the trick.

"It is one of those escapes which Houdini would not have hesitated to attempt," Walter Gibson wrote in *Houdini's Escapes*, a book Bess helped the author prepare after Houdini's death. "But the average escape artist would not undertake it, even though he knew the secret and had the appliances."

The Milk Can Escape quickly became the climax of Houdini's act. In cities where there were breweries, he reaped reams of publicity by challenging local brewers to fill the can with beer. In other cities, he challenged local dairies to fill the can with milk.

Eventually he made the escape even more popular by having the padlocked can placed inside an iron-bound wooden box, which was also padlocked.

"THE DOUBLE FOLD DEATH DEFYING WATER MYSTERY," he proclaimed on his posters. "FAILURE MEANS A DROWNING DEATH."

Houdini even tried to work out an escape where the milk can would be placed upside down in a larger, water-filled can.

"I am to be placed in one can in a standing position," he wrote in his notes, "this to be turned upside down into the larger can. . . . Both cans are locked."

He was never able to work out the Double Milk Can Escape well enough to perform it, however.

Houdini finished the 1908 season by packing theaters coast to coast. In another new stunt, he escaped from four hundred pounds of chains that had been wound around him and padlocked. On a return visit to Boston, he performed his Milk Can Escape for Harvard students and did an underwater escape in the Charles River.

Bess arrived late for the jump and was stopped by a policeman when she tried to push her way through the crowd on the pier. She protested that she was Houdini's wife, but the policeman replied, "You're the ninth wife of his that has tried to pass here in ten minutes. It'll take you a marriage certificate to get through these lines."

On August 10, 1908, Houdini and Bess sailed from New York City for another tour of Europe. He and his mother promised to write each other often, and his mother stood on the dock waving as the ship sailed away.

Even more fame awaited Houdini in the years ahead, but he would also suffer more injuries that would slowly wear down his body.

seven

The next few months saw Houdini perform in Germany, England, France, Ireland, and Scotland. He dropped the handcuff escapes entirely, except when they were part of some other stunt.

He had also discovered that audiences were fascinated if they could watch him while he struggled to get out of his bonds. He therefore started performing most of his feats in full view, rather than behind the cabinet and curtains.

His escapes from milk cans, all kinds of crates, straitjackets, and "insane blankets" (wet blankets wrapped and bound around violent people to restrain them) filled theaters to overflowing. Many swim champions challenged him to hold his breath underwater longer than they could, and Houdini loved taking on these challenges.

He even had a huge clock placed on the stage, so the audience could time the contests. In between performances he practiced holding his breath while lying on a sofa in his dressing room, routinely holding it more than three minutes.

In virtually every city where he appeared, workmen built what they thought were escape-proof crates and challenged him to escape from them. In Belfast, Ireland, employees of the Harland and Wolff shipyards made a chest out of timbers meant for a huge ship they were building. The ship was to be almost 890 feet long and as tall as an eleven-story building. But although it would carry over 2,200 passengers and crew, there would only be lifeboats for about 1,200. The ship's name was the *Titanic*.

The workers nailed Houdini in the chest they made from the *Titanic*'s timbers and waited confidently for him to admit defeat. Instead, he escaped in a few minutes, leaving the top of the chest still nailed shut.

The stunt generated so much publicity that twenty thousand people had to be turned away from the theater in the days that followed.

Houdini also jumped while manacled into rivers and harbors in England, Germany, and France. He dove into the Spree River in Berlin, Germany; the Mersey in Liverpool, England; and the Tay in Dundee, Scotland.

Not content with performing stunts that would

have satisfied almost anyone else, though, he sought even more danger. On July 1, 1909, he performed what has been called the most hazardous diving stunt of his career. It took place in the harbor at Aberdeen, Scotland, in a howling gale. The waves were so high that veteran fishermen refused to venture out. In the morning a man had drowned after being swept overboard from a fishing vessel as it entered the harbor.

The authorities tried to stop Houdini, but he persuaded a tugboat captain to take him out. Once he was in the harbor, he had a heavy chain pulled around his neck, across his chest, and fastened to his arms. Then his hands were cuffed behind his back.

While the boat bobbed wildly and the crew tried to stop him, he leaped into the sea. Eighteen seconds later he reappeared, free of the chain and cuffs.

All these outdoor stunts, added to the ones he performed in theaters, were beginning to take a toll on his body.

"The act I am now doing — first the straitjacket, then the can — is the hardest on my body that I have ever attempted," he wrote in his diary.

But he refused to slow down, seeming to believe

that his body could defy the rules that applied to everyone else. The secret of his success, he declared, was "vigorous self-training, to enable me to do remarkable things with my body, to make not one muscle or a group of muscles, but *every* muscle, a responsive worker, quick and sure . . ."

Houdini and Bess missed "the two mothers," and so he brought Cecilia and Bess's mother over to England for two months in the summer of 1909. He gave each one a daily allowance and spent all his leisure time showing them around.

The last show they saw him perform was in Plymouth. Employees from the government ship-yard nailed Houdini into a special packing crate, using two-and-a-half-inch nails.

The crowd, trying to see this latest challenge, was so large and unruly they smashed three of the theater's front doors. Police reserves had to be rushed to the theater to keep order.

Houdini used several methods in his escapes from packing boxes, but they all depended on making sure one side of the box was weak and could be opened. Jim Collins, who was an expert carpenter, was usually the assistant who figured out how to "fix" a challenge box.

Having a good assistant once the performance started was also "absolutely necessary . . . ," Houdini said. "He mingles among the committee as one of them and (unostentatiously) directs, assists and steers the committee from placing too many nails in the part of the box that the performer intends to direct his attention to when imprisoned."

The lid of the box was the last part nailed on and "should receive a liberal supply of nails," Houdini said, "as the audience's attention is drawn to same as the most invulnerable part."

Most people assumed that the top was the only way out, but Houdini never escaped through the top of a box. One of his favorite methods was crawling out through a specially hinged board near the bottom of one side. Audience members were amazed, therefore, when they saw the top still firmly nailed down after he escaped.

Members of the audience at Plymouth were so thrilled with his performance that they carried him to his hotel on their shoulders (though some people said Houdini arranged the "spontaneous" demonstration himself). He was especially proud that his mother had seen this moment of triumph, and wrote in his diary, "The two mothers and Bess at windows and hear 'em cheer me for ten minutes."

Mrs. Weiss and Bess's mother were scheduled to leave Southampton for the United States the next day. Although Houdini was tired and there was a heavy rain, he hired a car and drove all night to the port. He never let his mother leave after a visit without kissing her good-bye before she walked up the gangplank.

His strong attachment to his family was also shown every October 5, the anniversary of his father's death. No matter where he was, he would honor his father on that day by going to a temple and saying the mourner's kaddish, a Hebrew prayer for the dead.

On October 5, 1909, a few weeks after Cecilia left, he wrote in his diary, "Went to Manchester to a temple early at six o'clock, and said Kaddish. One man gave me a tallis [a prayer shawl]. Placed it over my shoulders."

The next month he traveled to Germany to perform at a theater in Hamburg. The performances went well, but the highlight of the trip occurred far from the theater.

One morning he saw his first airplane and immediately fell in love with it. For a man who had always been fascinated by mechanical inventions of all kinds, and who often called himself an inventor because of the locks and handcuffs he developed, the airplane was like a dream come true. It was called a Voisin, a biplane built by Voisin Frères in France, and Houdini arranged to buy it almost as soon as he saw it. He painted the word *HOUDINI* in bold letters on the sides and tail, bought the cap and goggles that aviators wore, and hired a French mechanic named Antonio Brassac to teach him to fly.

Wilbur and Orville Wright had given their first public flying demonstrations in Europe just one year earlier, and there were only a handful of airplanes in the world. All were awkward and fragile-looking, like big boxes nailed together.

The speed record in an airplane was only 47.1 miles an hour. Pilots had trouble getting them more than a few hundred feet off the ground, and the planes were as likely as not to crash.

But far from being turned off by the danger, Houdini loved it. He arranged for the use of a German army parade-ground as a temporary flying field, in exchange for teaching several German officers the fundamentals of flying.

After performing at the theater twice every night, Houdini rose early in the morning and hurried to the field. Strong winds kept him on the ground the first few days, but they finally died down.

He climbed into the Voisin, started its 60-horsepower engine, and managed to get the plane a few feet off the ground. Then suddenly it crashed, nose-first. "I smashed machine," he wrote in his diary. "Broke propeller all to hell."

That didn't discourage him, however, and as soon as the plane was repaired he flew it again. He was as excited as a child with a new toy, and had several photographs taken of himself seated in the plane surrounded by German officers.

There was, he declared, "magic in flight."

In early 1910, a few weeks after these first lessons in Hamburg, Houdini sailed for Australia with Franz Kukol and Bess. He also took along Antonio Brassac.

Houdini had always suffered from seasickness, but it had now gotten so bad that even the sight of a ship made him sick. He decided to risk the almost monthlong journey to Australia for three reasons: The promoter promised to pay him for the days spent traveling; he wanted to give his body a rest from the grueling strain it had endured for years; and, probably the most important reason of all, he wanted to go down in history as the first person to successfully fly an airplane in Australia.

Houdini had the Voisin packed in several large crates and stored in the hold of the ship. He also brought along an extra motor and several spare parts.

The first thing Houdini did when the ship reached Adelaide, Australia, in February, 1910, was stuff himself with huge meals to regain the twenty-eight pounds he lost during the voyage.

His performances in Australia drew large crowds, but they were nothing compared to the throngs that turned out to watch his manacled dives. His thirty-one-foot leap into the Woolloomoolo Bay in Sydney almost ended in disaster when he hit the water face-first, according to a reporter, and suffered "a terrific blow."

Although Houdini successfully hid his pain from the crowd, the dive gave him two black eyes and loosened several teeth.

An even more disquieting leap for Houdini was one into the Yarra River in Melbourne. Twenty thousand people watched as he disappeared, chained and padlocked, into the muddy waters. When he finally surfaced, he was startled to see a corpse floating a few feet away.

Houdini's plunge had apparently dislodged the corpse from the river bottom. Reporters said he was "frozen" by the sight, and had to be hauled into the waiting rowboat like a log.

He and Brassac assembled the Voisin at Diggers Rest, a field about twenty miles outside Melbourne. Houdini often slept at the field so he could begin working on the plane at dawn.

On March 18, the plane was ready and the winds had finally died down enough for Houdini to fly. A huge crowd watched as he made three flights. The longest lasted three and a half minutes, reached an altitude of approximately one hundred feet, and covered two miles at a speed of fifty miles an hour.

The crowd cheered wildly and Bess threw her arms around him when he landed. HOUDINI FLIES read the headlines in the Melbourne papers. One magazine wrote that his plane "was circling and whirring round like a gigantic bird."

"Never in any fear and never in any danger," Houdini wrote in his diary. "It is a wonderful thing."

The hastily formed Aerial League of Australia presented him with a trophy inscribed, "To H. Houdini for the First Aerial Flight in Australia, March 16, 1910."

The wrong date on the trophy is curious. Houdini may have had the date changed from March 18 to prevent a young auto mechanic named Fred Custance from claiming credit for the first successful flight. Custance had flown on March 17, one day before Houdini. But although he successfully completed three one-mile circles of the field during his first flight, he was only about twelve feet off the ground. On his second flight he reached an altitude of fifty feet, but lost control of the plane and crashed.

Even though it was questionable whether Custance's "flights" really qualified as flights, Houdini must have felt threatened by them. In the privacy of his diary he reassured himself, "First real flight in Australia."

For all the importance he gave to winning the title, he had only spent a total of about one hour in the air. And although he kept the Voisin for three more years, he never flew again. His desire to fly, like so many of his passions, left as quickly as it had come.

Houdini often went with little or no sleep during his Australian tour, and the brutal schedule was beginning to take its toll. He told one reporter shortly before leaving, "I have done things which I rightly could not do, because I said to myself, 'you must'; and now I am old at 36."

He and Bess left Australia in May 1910, and spent part of the summer in New York City. Houdini and his mother were especially pleased that they were able to celebrate her sixty-ninth birthday together.

In August, Houdini and Bess sailed for England. During the next three years he played two nine-month tours in Great Britain and the Continent, plus a yearlong tour and summers in the United States.

He had already achieved almost mythic status in England, and it seemed that half the country was trying to invent new challenges to defeat him.

Four officers at the Chatham Naval Base challenged him "to stand in front of a loaded Government . . . Steel Gun, to which we will secure you, insert a fuse which will burn 20 minutes, and if you fail to release yourself within that time you will be blown to Kingdom Come."

Houdini accepted the challenge, but the chief of police in Chatham refused to allow the fuse to be lit. Instead, the officers chained him to the mouth of the cannon, lashed his wrists to each other across his chest, and roped his feet into an iron ring nailed into the stage floor.

First Houdini kicked off his shoes and used his bare toes to untie the knots that bound his hands. Then he wriggled, twisted, and strained against the remaining ropes. There were still three minutes to spare when he freed himself from the last of them and leaped free of the cannon.

But even a challenge such as this was not enough for the restless Houdini. "I have tried through many a sleepless night," he wrote, "to invent schemes to make an audience appreciate some worthy effort of mine."

The more of a legend Houdini became, the more he tried to prove that the legend was true. He acted as if he was some kind of superman whose body could endure almost anything, but Bess knew better.

"Harry is worked to death," she wrote in 1911, "he looks so old, he is quite gray."

Houdini also knew his body needed relief from the constant strain, but he admitted that fact only in his diary and letters.

"Gee but it's hard to keep at it all the time . . . ," he wrote. "Very hard job. Must invent some new means of enlightening my labors."

In the fall of 1911 and into 1912, he toured several American cities in the East. His act consisted mainly of the Milk Can Escape, the straitjacket escapes, and whatever challenges were thrown his way.

While playing Boston, Houdini heard of a sea "monster" that had been caught by fishermen off Cape Cod. It may have been an elephant seal, or a cross between a whale and another mammal: One newspaper called it a "What-is-it?"

The lieutenant governor of Massachusetts challenged him to escape from it and he readily agreed. Twelve men hauled the huge "monster" corpse onstage. Houdini, shackled hand and foot, was pushed through a slit in the beast's stomach. Steel chains were wrapped around the carcass and snapped shut with padlocks.

Bess recalled years later that this feat was perhaps the only time Houdini panicked. Suddenly dizzy and choking from the chemical fumes that had been used to preserve the corpse, he frantically tried to kick his way out of the carcass.

Quickly regaining his composure, however, he methodically set about freeing himself from his shackles, then crawled out of the carcass. The ordeal had lasted fifteen minutes.

A few weeks later, while playing in Detroit, he accepted a challenge to escape from a large bag fastened by several heavy straps. The straps were drawn tight by a "gang of longshoremen." After the escape, Houdini had sharp pains in his groin and began urinating blood.

He had ruptured a blood vessel in a kidney and was told by a doctor to rest for several months.

"If you continue as at present," the doctor reportedly said, "you will be dead within a year."

"You don't know me," Houdini replied.

He canceled a few dates, went home to New York to rest for two weeks, then began planning more difficult escapes than ever.

At the end of the year, he sent a message to the doctor saying, "Still alive and going strong." He sent such messages to the doctor for the next fifteen years.

The kidney continued to bother him, requiring him to sleep on a special pad to ease the pain. A few months after the kidney injury, he tore a ligament in one side of his body.

Again, he refused to stop performing, even though the pain is said to have left him shaking and white-faced after a difficult escape.

Houdini was worried about the injuries, but

tried not to let Bess know it. He briefly tried to lighten the strain on his body by including several minutes of "animated pictures" in his act. These were films of him jumping from bridges or flying his Voisin, but the effort didn't last long.

"I want a performance by you," one manager told him, "not a cinematograph act."

Apparently Houdini also didn't like showing films instead of performing, for he soon came up with an escape the magazine *Scientific American* called "one of the most remarkable tricks ever performed." On the morning of July 7, 1912, he arrived at a pier on New York City's East River. Houdini had made sure there were several reporters waiting for him, along with so many spectators *The New York Times* said the pier "was crowded to suffocation."

He brought along a box made of thick pine and announced that he would escape from it after it was nailed shut, bound by heavy ropes and metal bands, weighted down with approximately two hundred pounds of metal, and tossed into New York Harbor.

The police refused to allow him to perform, though, so he talked a tugboat pilot into steaming farther out into the harbor. The reporters went with him, and fastened his legs and arms with handcuffs and leg irons. Passengers from a nearby ferryboat lined the railings to watch.

Houdini stepped into the box, which was so small he had to sit with his knees pressed against his chest. The lid was nailed down, and the ropes, metal bands, and weights applied. There were holes in the sides to let air in, but they would also let water in.

Houdini's brother Leopold (now Dr. Leopold Weiss) stood by with his medical satchel in case something went wrong. The box was dumped into the harbor where it floated with the top just barely visible. In less than a minute, Houdini's head broke the surface of the water. Spectators cheered and tugboats tooted their horns, as he smiled and waved.

The next day a headline in *The New York Times* declared, HOUDINI BOBS UP SMILING IN THE HARBOR, THE BOX BEING UNOPENED AND STILL NAILED AND ROPED.

He was performing at Hammerstein's Roof Garden in New York at the time. The escape brought so much publicity that a 5,500-gallon tank was installed onstage, and he repeated the stunt every night.

Years later, Houdini claimed that at the end of the first week, he asked to be paid in gold coins. According to him, he then drove home, dashed into his mother's room, and cried, "Mother, Mother, do you remember the promise I made Father years ago that I would always look after you? Look what I am able to bring you now! Hold out your apron!"

He said he poured the coins into the apron in her lap, in what was the greatest thrill of his life.

Whether or not the incident ever happened, or happened as he claimed, there is no doubt he remained extraordinarily attached to his mother throughout his life. Bess apparently was not always pleased with this attachment. He once tried to explain his feelings about his mother to Bess in a letter, reassuring her that "the two loves do not conflict. . . . I love you as I shall never again love any woman, but the love of a mother is a love that only a true mother ought to possess, for she loved me before I was born . . ."

In the fall of 1912, he and Bess sailed to England for another tour of Great Britain and the Continent. He had been experimenting for at least three years with what some experts have called his greatest escape: the Chinese Water Torture Cell (Houdini privately referred to it as "the Upside Down" or "USD").

The basic apparatus for the escape consisted of a heavy mahogany tank or "cell" about five and a half feet tall, lined with nickle-plated steel. The sides were made of tempered glass, so the audience could see through them. Together with ropes, clamps, pulleys, and other equipment, the apparatus weighed about three quarters of a ton.

While assistants filled the cell with water, Houdini walked onto the stage clad in a bathing suit. He lay down, and the assistants and audience members locked his ankles into a heavy wooden stock, then secured a steel frame over the stock. A machine attached to the frame by ropes then turned Houdini upside down and lowered him into the cell. There was so little room, his shoulders pressed against the sides and excess water spilled onto the stage. To complete the imprisonment, a steel lid was clamped over the top of the cell and padlocked.

Curtains were then drawn around the cell while the orchestra slowly played "Asleep in the Deep," and Kukol and Collins stood by with axes in case something went wrong.

Nothing did. Houdini stepped through the curtains in about two minutes, smiling and waving while water dripped from him and the audience roared its approval. The padlock and the apparatus were undisturbed.

The escape, wrote one newspaper, was "uncommonly astonishing and awe-inspiring. . . . A trick of incredible cunning."

"I believe it is the climax of all my studies and labors," Houdini wrote. "Never will I be able to construct anything that will be more dangerous or difficult for me to do."

The USD became Houdini's most famous and requested act for the rest of his career. Its secret was known only to a handful of people, however, and he never explained publicly how it was done.

He posted a challenge before every performance of the USD, which read, "$1,000 Reward. Houdini offers this sum to anyone proving that it is possible to obtain air in the upside-down position in which he released himself from this water-filled torture cell."

And even though he often performed the USD seven days a week and twice a day when there were matinees on Wednesdays and Saturdays, no one was ever able to collect the reward.

The next several months saw performances by Houdini in England, where he also helped found the Magicians Club and became its first president.

One of his first acts was to donate a portrait of himself to hang above the bar.

Although Houdini often traveled second- or third-class to save a few dollars, he quietly spent large sums of money to help the poor. Besides seeking out the neglected graves of magicians and paying to fix them up, one of his fist acts as club president was to start a fund for magicians who were down on their luck.

Despite his wealth and fame, he continued to be plagued by some of his childhood insecurities. One of these was his short height. As president, he had a specially carved chair made to use during club meetings so no one could look down on him.

The late spring of 1913 found Houdini back in the United States for a few weeks. He gave some performances, but spent most of his time with his family.

His brother Bill was in a tuberculosis sanatorium, and Houdini went to visit him. He was especially worried about his mother, though. She was now seventy-two years old, and was often troubled with stomach pains.

Houdini sent her to the Catskill Mountains for a rest, but that didn't seem to help. On July 6, two days before he and Bess were going to sail for

Europe, his mother asked him to take her to the cemetery to visit his father's grave.

Theo and their brother Nat went with them. When they arrived at the cemetery, Houdini said he was going to lie down on his father's grave to be close to him, but Theo talked him out of it.

The next day they all went to the Hoboken docks, where Bess and Houdini were going to board the German liner *Kronprinzessin Cecilie* (*Crown Princess Cecilia*; the name "Cecilia" may have been one reason Houdini chose to sail on it).

"Not the usual good feeling that we had for past sailings," he recalled years later.

Houdini was reluctant to leave his mother and was the last passenger to board the ship. Even so, he kept going back to her and kissing and hugging her.

Finally, she said, "Ehrich, vielleicht, wenn du zurück kommst, bin ich nicht hier" (Ehrich, perhaps when you return I won't be here).

He laughed and said she had made the same comment in the past. He was still reluctant to leave her, but she finally ordered him to go.

"Look, my mother drives me away from her," he told bystanders.

"No, no, but you must leave now," Cecilia insisted. "Go quickly, and come back safe to me."

Houdini hurried up the gangplank for the last time. As he did so, his mother called out for him to bring her back a pair of size six woolen slippers.

"All right Mama," Houdini replied.

The *Crown Princess Cecilia* docked in Hamburg, Germany, a week later, and Houdini and Bess caught a midnight train to Copenhagen, Denmark. There he performed at the Cirkus Beketow, before an audience that included two princes of the Danish royal family.

The next day, during a press reception, Houdini was handed a cablegram. It was from Franz Kukol, and told him his mother had died earlier in the day from a stroke.

Houdini fainted. When he came to, he cried out, "Mama — my dear little mother — poor little Mama."

That night his kidney gave him so much pain a doctor urged him to go to the hospital. But Houdini refused, and instead caught a train to Bremen. While waiting for the ship that would take him and Bess to the United States, he went to a store and bought the size six woolen slippers his mother had asked for.

On July 29, three weeks after saying good-bye to his mother on the pier in Hoboken, Houdini walked into the parlor in Harlem and saw her "sleeping in her last bed."

He sat by her body all night, gazing "upon her features so still and quiet, resting for the first time in 'Her Earthy Career.' Her work was never finished. Night simply interrupted her work, but now as I always told Her she would 'Rest for Ever.'"

The next day he took the woolen slippers that had been "her last request" and placed them in the coffin before it was lowered beside that of his father in Machpelah Cemetery.

For the next several weeks, "bowed down with grief," Houdini left the house only to visit his mother's grave. He had a black border printed on his stationery, and wrote poems to his mother.

Bess said he would waken in the middle of the night and call out for his mother. And sometimes he sat up and asked, "Mama, are you here?"

He finally returned to work, sailing back to Germany on the last day of August for another tour abroad.

"I who have laughed at the terrors of death," he wrote of the pain he felt, "who have smilingly leaped from high bridges, received a shock from which I do not think recovery is possible."

He would visit his mother's grave for the rest of his life, lie face down on it, and tell her of his hopes, dreams, and accomplishments.

But the man who prided himself on being the greatest escape artist in the history of the world would never escape from the shock of his mother's death.

eight

The next several months were among the most difficult in Houdini's life. He performed in Germany, France, and Great Britain, but was constantly haunted by the loss of his mother.

In Nuremberg, Germany, after opening at the Apollo Theater, he wrote in his diary, "Act works beautifully."

But a few days later, in a letter to Theo, he said "my very Existence seems to have expired with HER. My brain works naturally, and I try and scheme ahead as in the PAST, but I seem to have lost all ambition."

He canceled shows in Paris and took Bess to the Riviera for what was supposed to be a vacation. But he spent much of his time roaming a cemetery for gamblers who had committed suicide after losing all their money.

In London, according to newspapers, he again canceled shows "with the intention of retiring from the stage."

Houdini performing his great "Vanishing Elephant" trick at
the Hippodrome in New York City *(Library of Congress)*

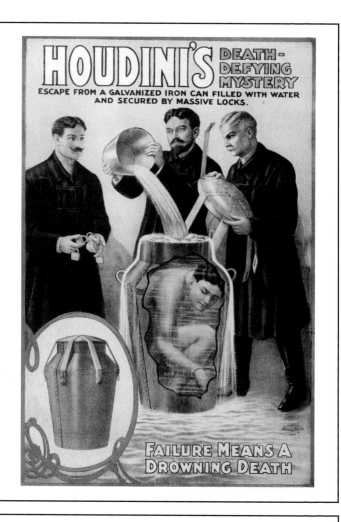

A poster advertising Houdini's famous "Milk Can Escape"
(New York Public Library)

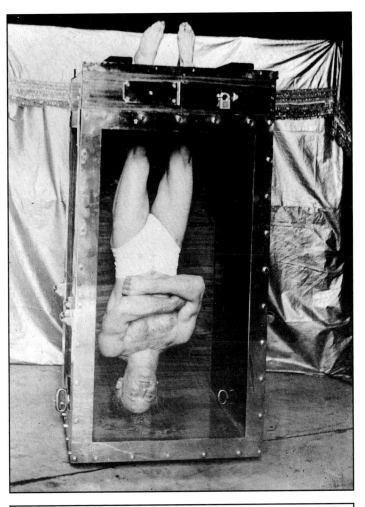

Houdini performing one of his most dangerous escapes from a device he called the "Chinese Water Torture Cell" *(Houdini Historical Center, Outgamie County Historical Society, Appleton, WI)*

Houdini with author, Jack London *(Brown Brothers)*

A poster from Houdini's first full-length motion picture, *The Grim Game,* 1919 *(The Everett Collection)*

A film still from one of Houdini's movies *(Houdini Historical Center Outgamie County Historical Society, Appleton, WI)*

Houdini in disguise, as an old man. It was by this method that he entered the homes of mediums and exposed fake séances. *(United Press International)*

Harry Houdini, "The man who walked through walls." *(The Everett Collection)*

But Houdini resumed performing and toured the English provinces. For the time being, he dropped most of the escapes that were becoming so hard on his body and presented a show that consisted almost entirely of magic.

Bess returned to the stage with him for the first time in years, and that lifted his spirits as they again performed Metamorphosis together.

"Bess working as though she had never retired," he wrote in his diary. "Best show I ever presented. Bess works magnificently."

He also enjoyed himself at meetings of the Magicians Club of London, although he had a humiliating experience one night.

The lights blew out and Houdini started for the cellar to check the fuse box. There was an old rusted padlock on the cellar door, and a friend held matches while Houdini tried to open the lock with his picks.

Try as he might, however, he could not open the lock and the meeting had to proceed by candlelight. When one magician kidded him about his failure, Houdini was so furious he yelled at the man for ten minutes. A friend said no one else ever dared mention the incident to Houdini again.

In June of 1914, he and Bess sailed for the

United States aboard the *Imperator*. One of their fellow passengers was former president Theodore Roosevelt, a fact that was to result in a brilliant publicity coup for Houdini.

People claiming to have contact with those who had died often "proved" their claim by performing what was called "spirit" writing. This consisted of having a spectator write a question on a piece of paper. The paper was then placed between two blank slates, together with a pencil that the "spirit" used to write the answer.

During a show for the passengers, Houdini asked Roosevelt to write a question for the spirits to answer. The question Roosevelt wrote was: "Where was I last Christmas?"

The ex-president placed the paper between the slates. When Houdini opened them, there was a map on the paper of the South American jungle where Roosevelt had spent the previous Christmas.

Roosevelt and the other passengers were amazed, and said the spirits must have drawn it. Houdini refused to give any explanation of what had happened. Years later, he said that when he learned that Roosevelt was going to be one of the passengers, he hurried to the *London Telegraph*. Houdini knew the paper had been publishing articles by Roosevelt about his South American expedition.

A friend at the paper gave him a map of the trip, which had not yet been published. Houdini also found out that the title of an upcoming Roosevelt article was "Celebrating Christmas at a Camp in the Andes."

When the performance began, Houdini tried to steer the conversation so Roosevelt would ask the spirits to tell him where he was last Christmas.

Whether because of Houdini's conversation, or because of pure chance, Roosevelt asked the question Houdini wanted him to ask. Houdini knew almost immediately what question Roosevelt had asked because he had placed a sheet of carbon paper under the cover of a book. Then he made sure the book was nearby so Roosevelt would use it to write on.

When Houdini reached over and took the book back, he turned his back to the audience, tore open the cover, and looked at the question on the piece of carbon paper.

"By a lucky chance it proved to be exactly the question I had prepared for," Houdini declared.

If it hadn't been that question, he would have

used sleight of hand to substitute a slip on which he had written "Where was I last Christmas?" That substitution would have looked like it had been placed there by the "spirits."

The next day when Roosevelt asked him whether the experience had been "genuine spiritualism," Houdini said he told him no, "it was hokus pokus."

"It can be readily seen why the Colonel was willing to believe that I possessed the power of drawing communications from spirits," Houdini said, "whereas I was simply resorting to a material experiment, in which, as it turned out, blind chance played a large part."

It was not entirely "blind chance," however. As Houdini himself noted about the supposedly impromptu performances he often gave, "In fact I sometimes prepare two weeks ahead for an impromptu show."

Ever conscious of the publicity value of any event, he made sure he stood next to Roosevelt in a photo that included several other passengers. Houdini then had the others airbrushed out of the picture so it looked like he and Roosevelt were standing alone as close friends. In the years to come, he mailed out countless copies of the photo.

While he had been aboard, Houdini had worked

out a stunt that is still legendary in the entertainment world: Walking Through a Brick Wall. The trick was a variation of one called "Walking Through a Steel Wall," whose invention had been claimed by an English magician. Houdini bought it from him and unveiled it publicly at Hammerstein's Roof Garden in New York City in July 1914.

While a packed audience watched, bricklayers constructed a wall onstage that was eight to ten feet high. It was built on a steel beam, which in turn rested on two-inch-high rollers at either end, so the wall could be rolled away after the act.

To make sure Houdini could not slip under the wall by using a trapdoor, it was built over a large, unusually thick rug, which was then covered by a sheet of cotton.

After being completed, the wall was rolled into position so that one end faced the audience. Houdini stood on one side of the wall while six-foot-high three-sided screens were placed around him. A three-sided screen was also placed around the side of the wall opposite him.

With the screens in place, the audience could still see the top of the wall. They could also see Houdini's hands when he waved from behind the first screen and shouted, "Here I am!"

Then his hands disappeared and he declared, "Now I'm gone."

The screen that hid him was instantly pulled away. No Houdini. Then the screen on the opposite side was pulled away, revealing a smiling Houdini who had apparently walked through the brick wall.

The audience was astonished and even some fellow magicians were at a loss to explain the trick. The explanation was simple, however. In spite of the fact that it seemed impossible for Houdini to go under the wall, he *had* gone under it.

"A large trapdoor was set in the center of the stage," Walter B. Gibson wrote in *Houdini's Escapes*. "When the screens were in position, the door was opened from below. Both the cloth and the carpet, which were large in area, sagged with the weight of the performer's body, allowing sufficient space for him to work his way through. . . . The passage accomplished, the trap was closed, and no clue remained."

World War I, which would last from 1914 to 1918, started shortly after Houdini returned to the United States. This meant he would not be able to perform in Europe for the next five years. He seemed uncertain what to do next, writing "the world looks and feels different since my Mother joined Her Best Friend and Sweetheart my Father."

In a strange choice of stunts, given his obsession with his mother's death, he accepted a challenge to be buried alive during an appearance in Los Angeles.

First he let the challengers handcuff him, then bury him in a grave one foot deep. He clawed his way up through the loose sandy soil. Then he let them bury him deeper and deeper, until finally he was under six feet of earth.

Through the years, he had thought nothing of being locked in boxes, tossed manacled into deep water, or locked upside down in water in the pitch darkness of the milk can.

But in the darkness of this grave, Houdini suddenly felt paralyzed by fear. He began to frantically claw the earth in a desperate attempt to reach the surface.

His strength began to fail and he tried to shout, but that only wasted precious breath and filled his mouth with sand. Finally he regained enough of his composure to methodically work his way up "and at last burst through into the sunlight, completely exhausted."

At about this time he also began performing another trick no one else had ever tried: escaping
while hanging upside down from the edge of a tall
building while bound in a straitjacket.

He performed the trick in almost every town he
appeared in for the next eleven years, reaping huge
amounts of free publicity and ensuring a packed audience for his theater performances.

One man who saw him perform the Suspended
Straitjacket Escape said his "rapid contortions
made it resemble a bag overcrowded with snakes
thrashing about in a death struggle."

Houdini was always fascinated by other men
who risked their lives, and had a special admiration
for professional fighters. On the night of November
30, 1915, while appearing at the Los Angeles
Orpheum, he noticed Jess Willard sitting in the first
balcony near the stage. Willard, who stood six feet
seven inches tall and weighed 265 pounds, was the
heavyweight champion of the world. Surprised and
pleased that he was present, Houdini invited him
down to the stage.

But Willard refused. According to Houdini, the
champion "half arose and was going to crush me
forever, blurting out in his gutteral voice, 'Go on
wid the show, you faker . . .'"

Houdini said he became "white with rage" and yelled back at Willard that "I will be Harry Houdini when you are not the heavyweight champion of the world!"

His reply, he claimed, sent the 2,300 spectators "stark, raving mad" as they vented their fury at Willard for ten to fifteen minutes.

All this time, Willard "shook his great fists at me and offered me a thousand dollars to come up to him, as he wished to annihilate me. But he could not make himself heard above the din . . ."

In describing the incident to his sister, Gladys, Houdini said he was afraid Bess would be angry with him when he came offstage. "But she was with me. In fact in all my fights when she thinks I am right she is alongside, helping me load the machine guns."

Newspapers throughout the country headlined the incident, leading a jubilant Houdini to declare: "I have received at least a million dollars' advertising space from this fray."

The same month that Houdini had his run-in with Willard, he met writer Jack London and his wife, Charmian. London loved to perform magic tricks for his friends, and was thrilled to meet Houdini. The hero of his most recent novel, *The Star*

Rover, had been a convict who was trussed up in a straitjacket.

Houdini, on his part, still felt ashamed of his limited education and longed to be accepted as an intellectual. By this time, in fact, he was proud to be corresponding with poets, writers, and scholars, including Robert Gould Shaw. Shaw was a Boston collector whose private library became the basis of Harvard University's theater collection. Houdini dreamed of eventually expanding his collection into serious literature so he could "take my stand with the other Drama 'guys' . . ."

He therefore eagerly accepted the friendship of London, author of *The Call of the Wild*, *The Sea-Wolf*, *White Fang*, and several other books, and one of the most popular writers of his time. A few days after their first meeting, Houdini had a photograph taken of himself and London. As usual with photos of himself and someone famous, he sent copies to friends.

Houdini always claimed he loved only two women in his life: his mother and Bess. But he and Charmian apparently felt an immediate attraction for each other.

"Charming Houdini," she wrote in her diary a few days after they met. "Shall never forget him."

Nor would he ever forget her. After Jack London died a few months later, they began a brief affair. Charmian London was about as different from Houdini's "Sweetie Wifie," as he often called Bess, as she could be. She had helped London sail his yacht to the South Pacific, and accompanied him to Mexico when he went to write about United States troops sent there during the Mexican Revolution.

Charmian called Houdini "Magic Lover," and he told her, "Now I know how kings have given kingdoms for a woman. You are gorgeous — you are wonderful. I love you."

Bess apparently knew nothing about the affair, and one can only guess at the inner turmoil the straitlaced Houdini must have felt. His private life seemed to consume as much energy as his theatrical life during this time. It had been almost three years since the death of his mother, but he said he still felt her loss "more and more as time goes on."

He also still grieved for his father, although Mayer Weiss had died almost a quarter of a century before. One of the first things Houdini did when he played at a new theater was to place a photograph of his father on the dressing-room table.

In 1916, he paid approximately forty thousand dollars to have a giant monument made for his mother at Machpelah Cemetery. It was cut from a thousand tons of Vermont granite, adorned with figures carved from Italian marble, and large enough to hold the entire family. A crowd of approximately 250 people attended its dedication.

Houdini seemed more fascinated than ever with death, which he called the "Great Mystery." In fact, his most difficult escapes had always been like deliberate challenges to death.

One writer said Houdini "was playing allegorical charades in which he died and was resurrected. He aroused the most primitive anxieties in his audiences. . . ."

Now he made pacts with various friends, agreeing that whoever died first would try to contact the one still living.

If he was in New York on the anniversary of his mother's birth or death, he always visited her grave. These visits were sometimes made at midnight or at dawn. He also made a practice of visiting his mother's grave on his own birthday, and even bought a bicycle especially for trips to Machpelah.

One year, in order to "make Her a birthday present," he had the body of his mother's mother disinterred and reburied beside her.

The entry of the United States into World War I

in 1917 finally began to bring Houdini out of his grief over his mother's death. Within weeks he signed up for the draft, declaring, "Hurrah, now I am one of the boys."

Houdini also quickly rearranged a few facts about his life, in an attempt to prove he was a full-blooded American. He claimed that his first flying lessons had been in Australia, although they had been in Germany. He also destroyed the photographs that showed him seated in his plane surrounded by German officers.

And he once again gave his birthplace as Appleton, Wisconsin, rather than Budapest, Hungary.

When the army turned down the forty-three-year-old Houdini because he was too old, he canceled several theater dates and entertained thousands of soldiers for free.

"My heart is in this work," he said, "for it is not a question of 'Will we win' or 'Will we lose.' *We must win*, and that is all there is to it."

One of his favorite tricks for the soldiers was "Money for Nothing," in which he seemingly pulled gold coins out of the air, then tossed them to the audience. He claimed he gave away about seven thousand dollars of his own money this way.

In honor of his father, he organized the Rabbis'

Sons Theatrical Benefit Association, which built a recreation center for soldiers on Long Island. Houdini was president of the organization, and the vice presidents were two other entertainers whose fathers had been rabbis: Irving Berlin and Al Jolson.

Within a few months, Houdini had helped sell more than one million dollars of Liberty Bonds. He also staged a huge benefit at the Hippodrome for the families of soldiers who were killed when the troopship *Antilles* was sunk by Germans.

The soldiers were the first Americans to die in the war. Houdini's benefit, which was staged on November 11, 1917, packed the 5,300-seat theater and raised almost ten thousand dollars.

He resumed his paid performances at the Hippodrome, but took time out during intermissions to teach soldiers how to break open locks, stay alive longer underwater, and escape from torpedoed ships. These sessions were "daily besieged by hosts of boys in khaki," declared the theatrical magazine *Billboard*.

Two months after the *Antilles* benefit, Houdini performed a trick that is still talked about today: the Vanishing Elephant.

He bought the rights to the trick from its British inventor, the illusionist Charles Morritt, who had been performing a "Disappearing Donkey" trick in England for years. But Houdini was not content with making a donkey disappear. Instead, he changed the illusion to feature the biggest creature he could think of — an elephant.

The elephant's name was Jennie, and Houdini told reporters she weighed over ten thousand pounds (privately he said she weighed about four thousand). At any rate, she looked impressive when she marched onto the stage of the Hippodrome "dressed up like a bride," as Houdini described her.

He fed her some sugar, kissed her, then had twelve men wheel an eight-foot-square cabinet onstage.

"The trainer marched the mammoth in a circle around his lodging house and then led the brute into it," a reporter wrote in *Variety*. "Curtains closed. Curtains opened. No elephant. No trap. . . . it had gone. . . . Mr. Houdini has provided a headache for every child in New York. . . ."

Houdini claimed the curtains were only closed for two seconds. At any rate they were not closed very long. Where did the elephant go?

She could not have gone through a trapdoor because the theater's giant water tank was beneath the stage, and it was filled with water.

Some fellow magicians pointed out that the stage was huge, the cabinet was placed just a few feet from the back and slightly elevated, and only a few of the thousands of spectators could see into the cabinet when the curtains were opened. Most of the audience had to take Houdini's word for what had happened.

Other observers pointed out that the trainer had vanished along with Jennie, meaning he had probably hurried backstage with her.

Houdini smiled at all the questions about the trick and said, "Even the elephant does not know how it is done."

The publicity that resulted from the Vanishing Elephant trick was all he could hope for. Although only a few thousand people could fit into the Hippodrome and only a handful of them could see into the cabinet, millions more read about the incredible man who could make an elephant disappear.

In addition to his performances and benefits for soldiers during the war, Houdini also found time to do what he called "Good Works." It was only right, he declared, "that what brains and gifts I have should benefit humanity in some other way than merely entertaining the people."

He gave money to the needy, arranged for the poor to attend his shows for free, and performed at orphan asylums, hospitals, and prisons. He even presented a special show for blind children.

In 1915, he performed before 1,700 men in the yard at San Quentin Prison, and, in 1916, gave a show and speech for 1,500 inmates at Sing Sing Prison.

One of his tricks at Sing Sing involved borrowing a watch, then breaking open a loaf of bread to reveal the watch hidden in the center. Much to Houdini's surprise, when he broke open the loaf, "two convicts grabbed the bread and ate it. It was white bread and I think they get only gray or black. . . . Next time I'll produce it in the midst of a pound cake."

As if his life was not busy enough, Houdini continued to be involved with Charmian London. Once he sent her a Mother's Day card filled with praise of his mother. Another time he said, "I would have told her — my mother — about you."

He apparently felt guilty about the affair, though, and often failed to make promised visits when she came to New York to see him. Charmian wrote in her diary that he was a "poor, sad, lonely thing."

After she returned to California, he phoned almost every day. But although he called and wrote her for the rest of his life, they met just once more.

His whirlwind schedule of theater performances and free benefits for soldiers continued until the war ended on November 11, 1918. By that time Houdini was ready to plunge into his latest obsession: making movies.

nine

By the end of World War I, movies were rapidly replacing vaudeville as the most popular form of entertainment for most Americans. Unlike many vaudeville performers who thought movies were just a passing fad, Houdini realized they were here to stay.

He was also quick to see them as a way to make money, to reach a vaster audience than he could ever reach in person, and to preserve his major tricks so future generations could see them.

"I think the film profession is the greatest," he said with the same passion he had shown in his brief love affair with flying, "and that the moving picture is the most wonderful thing in the world."

His first movie, which was produced by Octagon Films, Inc., was a fifteen-part action serial called *The Master Mystery*. It was silent, as all movies were at that time, and was shot at a studio in Yonkers, just north of New York City.

The movie featured Houdini as Quentin Locke, a secret agent for the United States Justice Department. Locke worked undercover as a laboratory technician at a huge, castlelike house owned by International Patents, Inc.

The owners of International Patents were villains who were trying to keep all new inventions from being produced so they could control the market with their own inventions.

Houdini had to fight off a robot called the Automaton. The Automaton was controlled by an evil genius, and in each episode he tried to kill Houdini a different way, from wrapping him in barbed wire to tying him at the bottom of an elevator shaft while the elevator slowly descended to crush him. As if that were not enough, the Automaton could also emit lethal electric rays through his fingertips.

For good measure, two love interests were thrown into the movie: Eva Brent (good woman) and DeLuxe Dora (bad woman). Houdini also had to traipse through several opium dens searching for a cure for Madagascar Madness, a disease from Asia that turned its victims into idiots who couldn't stop laughing.

His battles with the Automaton gave Houdini a chance to show off his skills at escaping. In one episode he broke out of a jail cell, while in another he clawed his way out of a pit filled with gravel and debris. He also managed to get himself nailed into a packing crate and tossed into the water.

During the course of *The Master Mystery*, Houdini escaped from a straitjacket, all sorts of manacles, and an underwater diving suit. He insisted on doing all the stunts himself, and managed to break three bones in his left wrist during the filming.

Houdini promoted *The Master Mystery* as enthusiastically as he had promoted his stage performances. In one day alone, he traveled to fifteen theaters in New England. His efforts paid off, and when the movie opened at the St. James theater in Boston, five thousand people had to be turned away.

Billboard published a review of the movie that sounded like it had been written by Houdini, predicting that "this cracker-jack production will thunder down the ages to perpetuate the fame of this remarkable genius whose unparalleled achievements have reached from Aroostock, Me., to Singapore, China, from Zululand to Behring Straits."

Few other reviewers were as enthusiastic, but the movie drew packed crowds throughout the United States. It was soon booked in countries around the world, and Houdini seemed convinced that fame and fortune awaited him as an actor.

"Movie Fans are 'clambering' for another Houdini serial," he said, "and . . . that is much easier than my Self-created hazardous work."

By 1920, forty million Americans were going to the movies every week, and the leading motion picture company was Famous Players-Lasky Corporation in Hollywood. Lasky movies featured the most popular stars of the day: John Barrymore, Mary Pickford, Rudolph Valentino, and Gloria Swanson.

Houdini signed with Players-Lasky for two movies at a reported salary of $2,500 a week, plus a percentage of the profits. He and Bess moved into a rented bungalow in Hollywood in the spring of 1919. It marked the first time in twenty-five years of marriage that they were able to stay in one place more than a few weeks.

Unlike *The Master Mystery*, which was a serial, the movies Houdini made for Lasky were feature films. The first one was called *The Grim Game*. It was another action thriller with a love interest.

The movie, which Houdini helped write, was packed with thrilling escapes. Audiences saw Houdini break out of a jail cell, free himself from a straitjacket while hanging upside down from a roof, and dive between the wheels of a speeding motor-truck and foil his pursuers.

But the most thrilling stunt in the movie was unplanned. One of the scenes called for Houdini to jump from the wing of one plane to the wing of another, in order to save the kidnapped heroine.

The two planes somehow became locked together about 2,200 feet in the air, and spiraled helplessly toward the earth.

Just when it seemed they would crash and kill all aboard, the planes separated and managed to land safely. In the movie, a bloody Houdini is shown climbing from the wreck, triumphantly holding the rescued heroine in his arms.

"I was helpless — but strangely unafraid," he said of the near-crash. "A lifetime passed in an instant. *The crash will come. I shall be gone. But it is not all. There is another life. There must be!* was the comforting thought in my head. But fate ruled otherwise.

"By a miracle we righted into a half glide . . . I was miraculously unhurt."

There was just one thing wrong with Houdini's story: He was on the ground the whole time. He had fractured his left wrist again doing another stunt a few days earlier and the director, Irwin Willat, insisted they hire a double for the plane stunt.

"Houdini thought he was going to do it," Willat recalled, "but he was a very intelligent man and gave me no argument when I told him he wasn't."

A scene showing Houdini climbing from one plane to the other was shot on the ground, even though he later autographed pictures of the stunt with the words, "About 4,000 feet in the air."

When Houdini traveled to New York City for the opening of *The Grim Game,* he offered a thousand dollars to anyone who could prove that the midair collision was fake. The collision was real, of course, so Houdini knew his money was safe.

In a book written after his death and based on Bess's recollections, she portrayed herself as rushing to the scene and helping pull him from the plane, "half suffocated from being buried in mud . . ."

Bess was apparently Houdini's equal when it came to valuing a good story more than the truth.

Critics generally liked the thrills in *The Grim Game,* but audience reaction was only fair. One problem was that even though he took great risks to do his stunts, other actors could accomplish the same effects through the use of camera tricks. Houdini's real stunts, therefore, didn't look any more convincing than the phony stunts found in other movies.

Another problem with Houdini's movies was his stilted acting, especially in the love scenes. He was so self-conscious that he kept glancing over at Bess anytime he had to kiss the heroine. Houdini apparently found it extremely difficult to kiss any woman but Bess — at least when she was watching.

None of the criticism seemed to trouble him, however, and he declared of his acting talents, "They say I am the most sincere actor on the screen." He also was gratified at finally being accepted, at least in his view, as part "of the dramatic profession . . ."

In the summer of 1919, Houdini and Bess celebrated their twenty-fifth wedding anniversary at a hotel in Los Angeles. He invited two hundred guests, including the humorist Will Rogers, and hired a band that played the Wedding March as he and Bess walked in.

He told Bess that night, "I love you — love you — and I know you love me. . . . Think dear heart, twenty-five years . . . yours till the end of the world and ever after. Ehrich."

In what he apparently thought was the highest compliment he could pay her, he added, "If only my Sainted Mother were here, how she would nod her head with pride."

Although he seemed sincere in his feelings for

Bess, Charmian London said she received two "love notes" from Houdini during this period.

Autumn found him making his second movie for Players-Lasky, a thriller called *Terror Island*. It was filmed off the coast, on Catalina Island. The plot called for Houdini to recover a case of diamonds from a sunken ship, do battle in a submarine that was being flooded, rescue the heroine from inside a safe, and save her father from a savage tribe.

That seemed like enough to occupy anyone, even Houdini. But the most exciting action occurred, not on film, but in his real-life attempt to save four men caught in a sudden gale.

Spotting their boat as it was being swept toward rocks and what seemed like certain destruction, Houdini leaped into the ocean and began swimming toward the boat.

The waters were too rough, though, and deep-sea divers who happened to be nearby rescued an exhausted and bleeding Houdini. A motorboat eventually succeeded in towing the boat to shore.

Houdini wrote in his diary that *Terror Island* was "Excellent." But critics said parts of the plot that were supposed to be serious were so ridiculous that audiences howled with laughter.

Not long after completing the movie, Houdini

went back to New York City. He spent much of his time sorting through the thousands of new purchases he had made for his ever-expanding drama and theater collection.

In addition to books, he also had photographs, posters, autographs, programs, letters, and other items in what he proudly called his "young Harvard collection."

It had been almost six years since he toured England and France, and theater managers now asked him to fulfill contracts he had signed before the war. *The Master Mystery* was extremely popular in England, especially among young people, and this helped spark renewed interest in his stage performances.

Houdini and Bess sailed for England in December 1919. He drew huge crowds, and was paid record amounts for his performances.

Houdini seemed more interested in his movie career than the stage, however, and filmed scenes in London, Edinburgh, and Paris for possible use in future movies.

He even took his movie camera to cemeteries, which he continued to visit almost everywhere he went. When he and Bess visited the grave of Lafayette, a magician friend who had died in a fire,

Houdini said, "We had brought flowers in pots. . . . I said, 'Lafayette, give us a sign you are here.'"

The pots immediately crashed to the ground. Houdini set them upright, and this time they crashed to the ground "with such force that the pots broke."

Houdini wanted to believe that Lafayette was giving him a sign, but finally concluded that a high wind had knocked over the pots.

In the years immediately following World War I, with its massive loss of life, millions of people looked for some way to contact their dead loved ones. Spiritualism, with its belief that such contact was possible, was especially attractive to them.

Houdini reportedly attended more than one hundred séances during his six months abroad. He longed to speak with his deceased mother, and mediums claimed she could speak through them.

But every time a voice came through that was said to be his mother's, Houdini knew it was only the voice of the medium saying whatever she thought he wanted to hear.

"Even after our numerous disappointments," Bess said, "whenever we visited a new medium, Houdini . . . [would] sit with a rapt, hungry look on his face that would make my heart ache . . . the séance would go on, the same guesses, the same trivial nonsense, the usual spook tricks that Houdini could do with his hands tied. The rapt look would fade . . . At his next visit to his mother's grave, I would hear him say, 'Well, Mamma, I have not heard.'"

Houdini's relationship with Spiritualism finally turned to anger: anger at the phony mediums he saw taking advantage of people and anger that he could not make contact with his mother. It was as if he kept pounding on a locked door, and was finally giving up hope that it would ever open.

He began making notes and collecting material for a book that would expose the fraudulent tricks of phony mediums. He bought every book on spiritualism he could find, and mailed reports on the séances he attended to his secretary in New York, John Sargent.

"Bought about a hundred spiritualism books from Bruce's — a great lot," Houdini wrote in his diary. "Collins made a box so I can take them in my travels and refer to them as I write."

In another entry he said, "Bess and I go to Bath. I buy a spiritualist library from Gregory."

The world's most famous believer in Spiritualism at the time was Sir Arthur Conan Doyle, creator of the fictional detective, Sherlock Holmes.

Doyle was a doctor who believed he had been born "for one purpose, to be the torch bearer of Spiritualism."

He had converted to Spiritualism in 1887, but did not become an evangelist for the movement until after the death of his son in World War I.

About a year after his son's death, Doyle said they communicated with each other through a medium in London.

"His voice sounded very intense and earnest before me," Doyle said. He claimed he went on to have several other visits from "my arisen son."

Houdini met Doyle in April 1920, and the two quickly became friends. Doyle was the kind of educated man Houdini admired so much and wanted to impress.

When Doyle told him he had ninety-six books on his desk, Houdini replied, "It may interest you to know that I travel with a bookcase containing over one hundred volumes, and recently, in Leeds, I bought two libraries on Spiritualism."

Houdini tried to hide his doubts about mediums and Spiritualism from Doyle, telling him, "I am seeking truth . . ."

The two men exchanged about ten letters in the first two weeks after they met.

"Am only too delighted to correspond with you," Houdini said, "and if there is anything in my little Kingdom of Knowledge that you wish to know, will only be too pleased to give you any information that I may possess."

By the time Houdini and Bess left England in July 1920, he felt that Doyle was "just as nice and sweet as any mortal I have ever been near." That opinion would change drastically in the years to come.

Soon after Houdini returned to the United States, he formed the Houdini Picture Corporation, and announced that he would make four movies a year. In reality, he made just two before the company folded: *The Man from Beyond* and *Haldane of the Secret Service*.

Houdini starred in both, and claimed that he wrote the script for *Beyond* in ten days. The plot seems driven by Houdini's need to somehow find a way around death. The movie closes with him reading a statement from one of Doyle's books on Spiritualism, *The Vital Message:* "The great teachers of the earth . . . have taught the immortality and progression of the soul."

And advertisements for the movie asked, "Dare you say there is no life after death?"

Audiences were not impressed by the message or the movie, at least not enough to make it the financial success Houdini had hoped for. And they were even less impressed by *Haldane of the Secret Service*. Houdini himself seemed to be tiring of the movies, and performed just one stunt as he battled a gang of counterfeiters in *Haldane*.

"Perhaps the renown of Houdini is fading," wrote a reviewer in *Variety*, "or more probably the Broadway managers were wise to how bad a film this one is . . ."

Houdini, who had thought he would become rich as an actor, lost thousands with his movie company and finally closed it. By the summer of 1922, he had been away from the stage for two years, except for one brief tour of the Keith circuit. He called that tour "probably my last engagement in vaudeville." Old injuries bothered him and he seemed tired of performing the strenuous escapes that had left him looking "ten years older than I am."

Houdini also knew that vaudeville was dying and that audience tastes were changing. A comedian and a singer were billed above him in one theater, while in another he had to share publicity with a cartoon and two short movie features.

But unknown to Houdini, while his career as the world's greatest escape artist seemed to be ending, he was about to embark on a second career that would prove just as exciting: as an investigator of Spiritualism and fraudulent mediums.

ten

In the months following his return from England, Houdini continued to attend séances and spent much of his time working on what he called his "spirit book."

He intended the book to reveal the tricks many mediums used to make people believe they were communicating with the dead. Titled *A Magician Among the Spirits*, Houdini hoped it would earn him a place in the literary world and be "part of my monument."

Earning a place in the literary world was increasingly important to Houdini. He continued to collect books and other materials, and finally hired a full-time librarian, seventy-five-year-old Alfred Beck, to arrange his growing collection.

Beck was an Englishman who had been in charge of the Harvard theater library for ten years, and also knew several leading writers and actors in the theater. Houdini seemed almost in awe of his background, and later said Beck was responsible for "what little knowledge I possess re history of drama."

Hiring Beck freed Houdini so he had more time to work on his book, but Beck was feeling anything but free as he organized the massive collection. He worked from early morning to late at night sorting the materials stored in several rooms in the Harlem brownstone. Houdini estimated the task would take a year, but he kept buying new materials and Beck ended up spending a year and a half on the job.

"Oh! what a task and time I have had on this collection," he told a friend. "It beats anything I have ever manipulated in my career, and I shall be most happy when I have finished the work."

In the spring of 1922, Sir Arthur Conan Doyle came to the United States to lecture on Spiritualism. He and his wife, Lady Jean Leckie Doyle, accepted an invitation to visit Bess and Houdini in Harlem.

Several weeks later, Bess and Houdini joined the Doyles in Atlantic City. Lady Doyle was said to be able to enter a trance and serve as a channel for spirits, who wrote messages using her hands. Doyle suggested that they hold a séance and try to contact Houdini's mother. Even while working on a book to debunk such communication, Houdini still wanted to believe it was possible.

Houdini agreed to the séance with Lady Doyle, and said, "I had made up my mind that I would be as religious as it was in my power to be. . . . I was *willing* to believe, even *wanted* to believe . . . with a beating heart I waited, hoping that I might feel once more the presence of my beloved Mother. . . ."

In fact, although Houdini believed in the spirit world, he had also come to believe that those who had died existed "on a plane so different from ours that they cannot possibly communicate with those on earth."

When Lady Doyle began the séance, Houdini said, she was "seized by a Spirit," her body shook, and she wrote fifteen pages of messages allegedly from his mother.

Unknown to Lady Doyle, the day happened to be the anniversary of Cecilia's birth, "my most holy holiday," Houdini said. Yet that fact was never mentioned.

He also noticed that the messages were in English, a language his mother almost never spoke, and that she failed to use any of her favorite phrases for him. And finally, Lady Doyle drew a cross at the top of the page when she began. Houdini was convinced that his mother, the wife of a rabbi, would never have drawn a cross.

Although he had no doubt of Lady Doyle's sincerity, he was convinced the messages did not come from his mother. He kept his doubts from the Doyles for the time being, but became more determined than ever to expose fraudulent mediums.

During a six-month vaudeville tour of the West, Houdini included tricks in his show that were used by phony mediums. Bells and tambourines would often sound in the darkened rooms where séances were held, without any apparent movement by the medium.

Houdini showed how he could produce these same "spirit" manifestations simply by hitting the bells and tambourines with his feet. This seemed impossible since his feet were held securely by volunteers from the audience. Houdini had a special hard shell built into one shoe, however, so he could withdraw the foot without the volunteers knowing.

When Doyle returned to England, Houdini exchanged letters with him every few weeks. But their differences were now apparent and the letters became increasingly angry, especially on Houdini's side. By the time Doyle returned for a second lecture tour, the two were feuding publicly.

Both happened to appear in Denver during the same week, and they met several times in an effort to revive their friendship, but it was too late. Newspaper stories quoted them attacking each other, though both men often claimed they were misquoted.

After one such story in a Los Angeles paper, Doyle wrote Houdini, "I am very sorry this breach has come, as we have felt very friendly towards Mrs. Houdini and yourself, but 'friendly is as friendly does,' and this is not friendly."

Although Houdini thought Doyle was sincere in his beliefs about spirit phenomena and communication with the dead, he declared, "There is nothing that Sir Arthur will believe that surprises me."

For his part, Doyle found Houdini a man of "strange contrasts."

After Doyle returned to England, Houdini wrote and asked for some information. Doyle refused to send it, replying, "You probably want these extracts in order to twist them in some way against me or my cause."

Houdini wrote once more, but his letter went unanswered. The two men never saw each other again.

Houdini's determination to expose fraudulent mediums had now become a crusade. Although he was the highest-paid performer on the theatrical circuit, he signed with a lecture bureau for much less money. The contract called for him to tour the Midwest and South giving twenty-four talks on Spiritualistic fraud.

"Whew!!!" he wrote in his diary. "Wait till Sir A. C. Doyle hears of my lectures."

He had already tried out the talks at the University of Wisconsin and the University of Notre Dame, where students and faculty enthusiastically applauded him.

Houdini, perhaps thinking of how proud his learned father would be of him, wrote in his diary that he was now "meeting the intelligentsa [sic]."

He exchanged letters with inventor Thomas Alva Edison, novelist Upton Sinclair, and writer/poet Rudyard Kipling, played golf with poet Carl Sandburg, and was visited by the literary critic Edmund Wilson.

A reporter in the *New York Herald Tribune*, reviewing one of his lectures, called Houdini "an amazing man . . . one of the most intelligent, I believe, of his time."

Houdini clipped the article and wrote at the top, "One of the best notices I ever had."

He spent much of the time in his lectures reproducing so-called psychic phenomena by using tricks he had learned as a magician, and drew packed houses almost everywhere he went.

Aware as always how to generate publicity, he challenged local mediums to take the stage and produce phenomena he couldn't duplicate. Sometimes these confrontations became almost violent.

In the fall of 1924, appearing in Denver, where the most famous medium was the Rev. Josie Stewart, Houdini spotted her in the audience and challenged her to come up "and deliver one message from the beyond."

Rev. Stewart refused to go onstage, but dared Houdini to come to one of her séances "and expose me if you can."

Houdini's voice trembled with anger as he continued to challenge her. Supporters of the two began exchanging insults, and the police gave Rev. Stewart a protective escort when she left the theater.

The next day a headline in the *Denver Post* read, HOUDINI STARTS NEAR RIOT.

Despite his demonstrations that there were natural explanations for the effects he could produce, many people were convinced that he possessed supernatural powers. Sir Arthur Conan Doyle, for instance, always believed there was no way Houdini could have escaped from the Chinese Water Torture Cell without dematerializing his body.

Houdini strongly denied any supernatural ability, though, and declared, "My methods are perfectly natural, resting on natural laws of physics. . . . I simply control and manipulate material things in a manner . . . equally understandable (if not duplicable) by any person to whom I may elect to divulge my secrets."

In the spring of 1924, the book he had researched for so long, *A Magician Among the Spirits*, was finally published (though Oscar Teale, a man Houdini hired as a researcher, said he actually wrote "the damnable work").

Magician, which included exposés of some of the leading mediums in the United States and Europe, was widely popular. But it also contained many factual errors and a vicious attack on Doyle, including excerpts from some of his private letters to Houdini. It ended any chance the two men had of renewing their friendship.

The lectures and publication of the book were exciting events for Houdini, but they also reminded him that his finances were getting dangerously low.

He always spent money almost as quickly as he earned it, and after all his years as a high-priced performer, he and Bess still had no savings.

On April 6, 1924, his fiftieth birthday, he wrote, "I am fifty years of age today and can't believe it. But I am! But not in body and far from it in mind. I believe if I live I'll be better, body and mind, than ever before, and more capable of making a living in my old age. But I must provide now!"

He continued to spend large amounts of money on his collection, however. Although he estimated that he already possessed a quarter of a million manuscript pages, Houdini bought the forty-six-year correspondence of an opera house in Cedar Rapids, Iowa (an estimated 25,000 letters) and enough posters from a lithograph company that went out of business to fill a five-ton truck.

Needing to replenish his bank account, he went on tour in the West in the fall of 1924. There his off-stage performances were as impressive as those he gave onstage. Discovering that a Los Angeles news-paper had run photos of two minor performers appearing on the same bill, but failed to run one of him, he raced into their office and "raised hell."

"All wrong on my account," he wrote in his diary,

"<u>but I could not help it.</u> I was so sore. I was so sore I had a headache all that afternoon."

And when Houdini discovered that a business was apparently using his name for its publicity value (the Houdina Company), he charged into the office and tore one of its name tags from a packing case. Newspaper reports said that when he refused to return the tag, four men tried to stop him from leaving and he began smashing their furniture.

Houdini's version, as usual, was even livelier. According to him, the four "Gorillas" were going to kick [him] insensible, cripple [him], and send [him] to the hospital.

He picked up the chair in self-defense: "Had no idea I was smashing up chandeliers. All I thought was to save myself. I picked up a chair and acted in real life the scenes that I have portrayed before the camera."

It later turned out that the Houdina Company was named for the man who owned it: Francis Houdina.

The subject of Spiritualism and mediums was now one of the most popular in the United States. Newspapers throughout the country routinely ran articles about mediums, as well as Houdini's challenges to them. Scarcely a day passed that his name was not mentioned in editorials, letters to the editor, and articles about the subject.

Whereas he had once been thought of solely as an entertainer, many now considered Houdini an expert on religion and science.

In a move that would lead to one of the most intriguing and widely reported episodes of his life, Houdini accepted an invitation to serve on a committee investigating mediums. The committee was sponsored by the magazine *Scientific American*, and offered a $2,500 reward to any medium who could produce psychic phenomenon — a "spirit photo" or a communication from the "spirit world" — under strict conditions.

The "Margery Case," as it came to be called throughout the United States and much of the world, was about to begin.

Margery, whose real name was Mina Crandon, was the beautiful, young wife of a Boston surgeon. Her supporters said she could go into a trance and deliver messages through the voice of her deceased brother, Walter.

"Walter" also announced his presence in other ways, including dragging a piano stool across the room, starting and stopping a grandfather's clock, tilting a table and rapping on it, ringing a bell encased in a wooden box, and tossing a megaphone through the air.

Houdini joined other members of the committee at a séance with Margery on July 23, 1924. The other members had already held more than fifty séances with Margery, and were largely convinced of her powers.

Speaking of Houdini's involvement in the case, *The New York Times* commented that "a gentleman who knows everything about legerdemain makes them (the spirits) very uncomfortable."

The first séance Houdini attended was held, as usual, in a dark room. He sat on Margery's left and her husband sat on her right (one of Walter's requirements for the séances was that Dr. Crandon always hold Margery's right hand).

To make sure she couldn't move and perform some of "Walter's" feats herself, Houdini held her left hand and pressed his right foot against her left foot. The box holding the bell "Walter" rang was on the floor between his legs, and the bell could only ring when a flap in the box's cover was pressed down.

Unknown to anyone else, Houdini had prepared for the séance by wearing a tight rubber bandage on his right leg all day. This made the leg extremely sensitive when he removed the bandage, and he was certain he would be able to feel the slightest movement of Margery's leg or foot.

The séance had barely begun when "Walter" announced his presence by whistling. Then he began to talk. As the session progressed, he threw over a cabinet, tossed a megaphone through the air, and rang the bell several times.

After the séance was over and Houdini was riding back to his hotel with two of the other members, he declared confidently, "I've got her. All fraud."

He said he could feel her slowly move her foot "to a point where she could get at the top of the box," and begin ringing the bell.

"I positively felt the tendons of her leg flex and tighten as she repeatedly touched the ringing apparatus. . . . Then, when the ringing was over, I plainly felt her leg slide back into its original position . . ."

Houdini said she had thrown over the cabinet by sliding her foot under it when the committee member on her right left the room, thereby freeing up her right foot and leg.

"Then she threw the cabinet over with her right foot," he said. "As she did so I distinctly felt her body give and sway as though she had made a vigorous lunge."

She managed to put the megaphone on her head at about the same time, Houdini said, and then "it was easy and simple for her to ask me or any one else to hold both of her feet and also her hands, and still she could snap the megaphone off her head in any direction requested."

The next night another séance was held. This time, when the table began to shake, Houdini moved his hands underneath it and felt Margery's head as she tipped the table.

"I do not think she was more surprised than I," he declared.

He wanted to publicly announce that she was a fraud, but other committee members decided to hold more sittings with her. This was done in August, but the members still failed to reach a decision.

Newspapers from coast to coast now ran front-page stories praising Margery or denouncing her. Comments about Houdini's involvement were often derogatory and sometimes ugly. One magician, referring to his well-known ego, said, "Every magacian [sic] in this country would like to see Houdini BEAT in the *Scientific American* Psychic prize."

J. Malcolm Bird, associate editor of *Scientific*

American and one of the committee members, believed in Margery's powers and intensely disliked Houdini.

"Houdini is a Jew," he wrote, as if that justified his anger at him.

At one séance, "Walter" sang, "Harry Houdini, he sure is a Sheeny."

And Margery's husband, Dr. Crandon, said he was sorry "this low-minded Jew has any claim on the word American."

In the fall, while the committee continued to debate what to do next, Houdini embarked on a tour of the West. He performed several of his old tricks, including the straitjacket and trunk escapes.

In San Francisco, he met Charmian London again for the first time in years. He and Bess invited her to dinner, but she turned them down. When Houdini called the next day and asked to come to her apartment, she quickly agreed. He never showed up, however, and Charmian wrote in her diary, "Meet planned & I wait alone in apt., & finally sorrowfully leave."

"Keep thinking of Magic," she said after he left San Francisco. He wrote her several weeks later, but they never saw each other again.

The great Margery debate continued to play

itself out. In December, Dr. Crandon accused committee members of trickery. In reply, Houdini offered to give five thousand dollars to charity if he failed to publicly duplicate any effects Margery could produce.

In the midst of all this, "Walter" announced that the spirit world had told him Houdini was going to die within the year. Other mediums also predicted his death, leading Houdini to declare that if he did die within a year it would simply be a coincidence.

On Christmas Eve, he took time out to give what had become his annual show at Sing Sing. The inmates nailed him into a packing case and he was out in twelve minutes, with the case still nailed shut.

He also took time out to visit an old friend who was now an inmate. Charles Chapin, former city editor of the *New York World,* had been convicted of murdering his wife of thirty-nine years by shooting her in the head while she slept.

Chapin had lost all his money and said he wanted to spare his wife a life of poverty. Houdini promised to visit Chapin whenever he had the time.

On February 11, 1925, the committee finally voted to deny Margery their $2,500 prize.

"We have observed phenomena, the method of production of which we cannot in every case claim to have discovered," they wrote in *Scientific American.* "But we have observed no phenomena of which we can assert that they could not have been produced by normal means."

Houdini was furious that the committee's denunciation of Margery was not stronger, declaring: "I contend that she is fraudulent in all of the manifestations that I have witnessed."

As with so many of the incidents in Houdini's life, however, the Margery case was not as clear-cut as he wanted it to be.

Houdini had his assistant, Jim Collins, build a special "Margery Box" for some of the séances. This was a cabinet that almost completely enclosed her so she couldn't ring the bell or perform the other manifestations attributed to Walter.

During one of the séances, Houdini "discovered" a folding ruler hidden inside the cabinet. He charged that the ruler had been planted there by Margery so she could use it to reach out and ring the bell.

Margery and her husband accused Houdini of planting the ruler in order to discredit her. Houdini vehemently denied the charge. He even had Collins come into the room and swear "by the life of his mother" that they knew nothing about how it got into the box.

Years later, however, Collins reportedly said of the ruler, "I chucked it in the box meself. The Boss told me to do it. He wanted to fix her good."

Whatever tricks he may have used, Houdini seemed confident that he had exposed Margery as a fraud.

"It takes a flimflammer to catch a flimflammer," he said.

With his fame more widespread than ever, Houdini was now about to enter the final phase of his career and of his life.

eleven

Houdini used his experiences with Margery and other mediums to make his stage presentations more popular than ever. Opening at the Hippodrome in New York City in early 1925, he demonstrated the tricks used by phony mediums to fool the public.

He also continued to perform many of his old feats, such as the Chinese Water Torture Cell and the trunk escape, but the "spirit" section of his show quickly became known as "the most remarkable and interesting act of Houdini's career."

In the show, Houdini invited several members of the audience onstage and blindfolded them to simulate a darkened séance room. He then asked them to hold his hands securely so he couldn't move them. While they did this, he easily managed to ring bells and tambourines by using his toes.

Houdini also performed other "spirit" manifestations, which totally confused the blindfolded men. The audience could see exactly how he was accomplishing the tricks, however, and roared with laughter.

Houdini's life now seemed almost consumed by his determination to expose phony mediums. The money they made, he declared, was "the dirtiest money ever earned on earth."

He urged judges to help pass legislation outlawing séance fraud, tried to interest President Calvin Coolidge in starting a government investigation, called on reporters to help him in his crusade, and even taught a course on séance fraud at the New York Police Academy.

After playing the Hippodrome, Houdini embarked on a five-month tour of the country. In a move that was as brilliant for its publicity value as any he had ever made, he sent private agents ahead of him to investigate mediums in every city he was going to play — "my own secret service department," he called them.

Houdini's lead investigator, a young woman from Brooklyn named Rose Mackenberg, later estimated she attended at least three hundred séances for Houdini.

Seeking out the town's leading mediums, the agents posed as clients trying to contact deceased loved ones. They usually named someone who had never existed, but the mediums invariably contacted them anyway after being paid. Upon learning the methods used by the mediums, the agents reported back to Houdini.

After he arrived in a city, Houdini used the information to expose any mediums who were foolish enough to attend his show. He also visited many of the mediums, disguising himself as a feeble old man and taking along a reporter and a prosecutor or detective.

He tried to trap one man, Pierre Keeler, for six years. Houdini finally succeeded with the help of his niece, Julia Sawyer. For a fee of three dollars, Keeler gave Julia spirit messages from her deceased sister. The only problem was that Julia never had a sister.

After her session with Keeler, Julia talked him into going outside to meet her aged Uncle Bill and his nurse. "Uncle Bill" was Houdini wearing a phony white beard and the nurse was a reporter.

When Houdini ripped off his beard, the startled Keeler cried, "Houdini, let me down easy! We're both in the same line."

His exposure of fake mediums drew headlines wherever he went, and many newspapers carried articles written by him about his experiences.

Despite this success, however, it seemed that thoughts of death continued to haunt Houdini. When his brother Bill died of tuberculosis, he wrote in his diary, "Slowly his wooden home was lowered into Mother Earth's breast. Asleep near his own mother, my mother. . . ."

Houdini made out his will, and the family plot figured prominently in it. He told exactly how he wanted to be buried: beside his mother. He also denied burial in the plot to his brother Leo. Years before, Leo had married the ex-wife of their brother Nat just ten days after she divorced Nat. Houdini was so enraged by Leo's action that he cut his head out of a family photograph. Now he specified in his will that Leo could not be buried in the family plot. For Houdini, with the value he placed on the family being together even in death, this was an act of ultimate anger.

He was also beginning to feel his age. "Can't believe I am so old," he wrote. "I feel so young — only I feel tired."

Bess tried to get him to rest during the summer of 1925, but he was too busy lecturing, tracking down phony mediums, and planning a big new show for the fall. He did much of the planning while taking long walks.

According to his niece, Mary Hinson Blood, Houdini would become so lost in thought during these walks that he would forget about everything else.

The new show Houdini came up with was the most ambitious he had ever done. It was called *Houdini* and consisted of two and a half hours divided into three parts: Act I was devoted to magic and illusions; Act II consisted of his most famous escapes; and Act III, titled "Do the Dead Come Back?", was a full hour of his Spiritualism exposés and lectures.

The show opened in Pittsburgh in the fall of 1925, then moved on to cities throughout the East and Midwest for the next nine months. Houdini offered a reward of ten thousand dollars to any medium who could perform a feat he couldn't duplicate. No one ever collected the reward.

He also continued to disguise himself as an old man and expose mediums during their séances. There have been suggestions that some of the mediums, wanting the publicity and certain that nothing could shake the faith of their followers, were paid by Houdini to let him "expose" them. Whatever the truth of this charge, the exposures always received great publicity in the newspapers.

During his ten-day run in Baltimore, for instance, Houdini made front-page headlines every day. Beginning with HOUDINI TO EXPOSE BALTIMORE FRAUDS and ending with HOUDINI'S OFFER STILL UNCHALLENGED, most of the articles were accompanied by photographs of him performing various escapes.

In the face of this massive publicity, no one seemed to notice or care that Houdini failed to expose a single medium in Baltimore.

In early 1926, Houdini was invited to Washington, D.C., to testify before a congressional committee investigating fortune-tellers. During four days of testimony before a packed, unruly crowd, he tried to convince the congressmen to pass a bill making it a crime to accept money for "pretending to tell fortunes . . ."

Many mediums were in the audience, and they constantly yelled, hooted, and insulted Houdini. Many shouted "Liar!" whenever he spoke, and they called him everything from crazy to a secret agent of a Jewish conspiracy to destroy Christianity.

After hearing himself called crazy and brutal, Houdini called on Bess to testify to his good character.

"Outside of my great mother, Mrs. Houdini has

been my greatest friend," he said. "Have I shown traces of being crazy, unless it was about you?"

"No," Bess replied.

Despite Houdini's efforts, the bill was not even reported out of committee.

Back in New York City, Houdini suddenly found himself about to undergo what was probably the most strenuous feat of his career. It all began when he heard of a twenty-six-year-old "Egyptian Miracle Worker" named Rahman Bey.

Bey, who was probably Italian, claimed to have supernatural powers that allowed him to go into "cataleptic trances" and stay alive while buried in a coffin under a mound of sand. In July, after Bey was sealed inside a coffin for one hour (almost half that time while the coffin was submerged in water), he challenged Houdini to do the same.

Houdini's goal in his underwater stunts had always been to escape as quickly as possible, not to stay down as long as possible. Bey's challenge angered him, though, and he quickly accepted it.

"I guarantee," he wrote in reply to Bey's challenge, "to remain in any coffin that the fakir does for the same length of time he does, without going into any cataleptic trance."

Houdini had a coffin built especially for the attempt, and practiced in the back room of a casket company. Hoping to use knowledge gained from the experience to help people trapped underground, he offered to share information from his experiments with the U.S. government. His offer was readily accepted by a physiologist for the U.S. Bureau of Mines, as well as by several manufacturers of mine-safety equipment.

For his first test, Houdini had a glass top placed on the coffin so he could be watched, and he lay down inside the coffin without having it submerged. For the second test, he had the coffin sealed with thirty-two bolts, lined with galvanized iron, and submerged under an inch and a half of water.

He also installed a telephone and safety bell in the coffin, in case he ran into trouble. In both tests, he was able to remain inside the coffin an hour and ten minutes.

The actual challenge took place on August 5, 1926, in the swimming pool of the Hotel Shelton. While a crowd of friends, reporters, and doctors stood three deep around the pool, Houdini was sealed into a new galvanized iron coffin six and a half feet long and about two feet high and wide.

Doctors present estimated there was only enough

air in the coffin for him to breathe about fifteen minutes.

"If I die, it will be the will of God and my own foolishness," Houdini said just before the lid was locked. "I am going to prove that the copybook maxims are wrong when they say that a man can live but three minutes without air . . ."

It took several tinsmiths eight minutes to solder down the lid. Teams of assistants then took turns sitting on the coffin to keep it submerged. The phone enabled Houdini and Jim Collins to communicate, but Houdini wanted to save his breath and said almost nothing.

For the first half hour, Collins announced the time to him every five minutes, then began announcing it every minute.

The water in the pool was warmer than Houdini expected and the temperature inside the coffin rose to almost 100 degrees Fahrenheit. His time underwater reached one hour and twenty-eight minutes. Perspiring heavily and feeling that he was about to lose consciousness, he ordered Collins to wait until he had been underwater an hour and a half, then haul up the coffin. He wanted to beat Bey's record by as much as possible.

Collins waited anxiously for the last two minutes

to tick by, then had several men haul the coffin out of the water. The tinsmiths ripped open the lid and Houdini climbed out, covered with perspiration and looking "deathly white."

He had beaten Bey's record by half an hour, leading *The New York Times* to declare, "HOUDINI WINS." Houdini went even further than the *Times*. With his usual enthusiasm for his own accomplishments, he printed up advertisements that read, "Buried Alive! Egyptian Fakirs Outdone. Master Mystifier Houdini 'The Greatest Necromancer of the Age — Perhaps of All Time.'"

"I deserve a rest," he said after the Shelton pool adventure, but spent the rest of the summer making plans for taking an improved version of *Houdini* on the road in the fall.

He also had a bronze coffin made to use in a new stunt for the show, and talked about taking a freshman English course at Columbia University when he had the time. He wanted to write a book about superstition that would be accepted by scholars, but still felt embarrassed by his lack of formal education.

"I have not a college grades nor possess degrees," he said, "and therefore it may not be taken as serious as I would like it to be."

In September 1926, he began the last tour of his life. Still wanting to prove that he could escape from what seemed like certain death, he had himself locked in the coffin. It was then lowered into a vault with a glass front so the audience could see inside. While they watched, about a ton of sand was poured into the vault. The coffin was almost totally buried, but Houdini managed to escape in just two minutes.

The first week in October, Houdini took his show to Providence, Rhode Island. Bess was stricken with ptomaine poisoning and became so feverish that Houdini sat up with her all night.

The next day, which was their last in Providence, he supervised the packing of their equipment for Albany, New York, their next stop. It was after midnight when he finished. He arranged for a nurse to accompany Bess to Albany, then hurried to New York City for several business appointments.

In the evening he went to the home of his lawyer, but the lawyer and his family had not returned from a trip to the country. Houdini lay down to wait for them, the first time he had been able to lie down in almost three days. In just twenty minutes the family returned, however. Houdini and the lawyer discussed several business affairs, then he remembered other errands he had to run.

About two o'clock in the morning, according to his friend and fellow magician, Joseph Dunninger, Houdini called and said, "I want to move some stuff from the house. Can you come up with the car?" Dunninger told him he was on his way.

It was raining hard when Dunninger arrived and Houdini was standing in the doorway waiting for him. They packed several piles of newspapers and magazines into the car, then Dunninger began to drive away. They had gone just a few blocks, he said, when Houdini cried out in "a hollow, tragic voice, 'Go back, Joe!'"

Dunninger drove back and Houdini stood looking at the house for a long time. Then he returned to the car and began to cry.

"I've seen my house for the last time, Joe," Houdini finally said. "I'll never see my house again."

It was almost four A.M. when he caught a train for the three-hour ride to Albany. He was exhausted when he arrived, but slept only about an hour before plunging into preparations for the evening show. He wanted to do especially well because he was told Governor Alfred E. Smith might attend.

That evening, while being lifted feet-first for the Chinese Water Torture Cell, his left ankle snapped. A doctor in the audience examined him and said it was fractured. He urged Houdini to go to the hospital right away, but Houdini refused.

"Nothing doing," he said. "They paid their money, and I'll see the show through."

He finished the show, limping painfully and spending much of his time sitting in a chair. Afterward the doctor applied a splint, and that night Houdini made a special leg brace to enable him to continue the tour.

He sent a message to the manager of the theater in nearby Schenectady, his next stop. According to the manager, Houdini said "that the accident [he] received at Albany Monday was only slight and that [he] will appear here as scheduled giving [his] show in its entirety."

Houdini not only completed three days of shows in Schenectady, but lectured before the student body at Union College and gave a speech on the local radio station.

His next stop was Montreal, Canada. He arrived there on October 18 with a "drawn face and dark shadows under tired eyes."

The next day he lectured to students at McGill University at the invitation of the head of the psychology department. His topic was "The Psychology of Mediumship." That night Houdini made the last entry in his diary: "Spoke for an hour, my leg broken."

One of the students at the lecture, Samuel Smilovitz, made a sketch of him. That night, after the evening performance, Smilovitz showed it to Houdini. He autographed it and asked the student to come to his dressing room the next morning to make a sketch for his own collection.

They met in the dressing room at about 11:30 A.M., along with a friend Smilovitz had brought along named Jacques Price. While Houdini lay on a small couch, Smilovitz began sketching him. He said later that Houdini looked tense and like a man "much in need of a long, carefree vacation."

After a few minutes a student named Whitehead arrived, and Houdini invited him in. Whitehead was over six feet tall and weighed about 180 pounds. He immediately began peppering Houdini with questions.

Then, "out of a clear blue sky," according to Smilovitz, Whitehead asked Houdini, "Is it true,

Mr. Houdini, that you can resist the hardest blows struck to the abdomen?"

At first Houdini ignored the question, but Whitehead persisted. Finally he asked, "Would you mind if I delivered a few blows to your abdomen, Mr. Houdini?"

Houdini gave permission and began to stand up when Whitehead hit him in the stomach with a "terribly forceful, deliberate, well-directed" punch.

"Hey, there," Jacques Price cried out after Whitehead hit Houdini again. "You must be crazy! What are you doing?"

Smilovitz said Whitehead continued to punch, landing two or three more blows before Houdini managed to raise his hand and mumble, "That will do."

Smilovitz and Price were stunned, and Houdini must have been in terrible pain. But he sat back down and allowed Smilovitz to finish his drawing. When it was done and the student handed it to Houdini, he commented, "You made me look a little tired in this picture. The truth is, I don't feel so well."

After the show the next night, Houdini was in so much pain he was unable to dress himself. He was scheduled to perform in Detroit the following day, and somehow managed to board the train with Bess and his assistants. He had such severe stomach pains, however, that a doctor was asked to meet him at the station in Detroit.

Houdini's temperature was 102 degrees when he arrived. The doctor wanted to put him in the hospital immediately, but Houdini refused. Instead, he checked into a hotel, then went to the theater for his opening performance.

His temperature rose to 104 degrees just before the show started, and every movement must have been pure agony. But he went through the almost hour-long first act smiling broadly as he tried to hide his pain.

Houdini collapsed offstage after the first act, but was revived and somehow managed to complete the show. He was so weak, however, that one of his assistants had to finish two of the tricks for him.

He returned to the hotel after the performance and refused the strong recommendation of the hotel's house physician that he enter the hospital. Finally, in the middle of the night, the pain became so great that Houdini agreed to go.

The next afternoon doctors removed his appendix, "a great long affair, which started in the right lower pelvis where it normally should, extended across the midline and lay in his left pelvis . . ." said one of them.

The appendix was gangrenous and had ruptured, flooding his stomach and organs with advanced peritonitis. He may have suffered from appendicitis even before being punched. In an age when there were no antibiotics, the poison of peritonitis was almost invariably fatal.

Houdini fought back, but on October 29 he was operated on again for "paralysis of the bowels." Bess visited him and he is said to have told her a message he would give her from the other side if he died.

"Mother never reached me," he reportedly said to her. "If . . . anything happens . . . you must be prepared. Remember the message: *Rosabelle, believe.* When you hear those words . . . know it is Houdini speaking. . . ."

"Rosabelle" was one of the songs the teenaged Bess had sung in her act at Coney Island when she and Houdini met.

Theo hurried to Detroit and Houdini made his final comment to him: "I can't fight any more."

On October 31, 1926, at 1:26 P.M., Houdini died. It was Halloween Day.

His assistant, Jim Collins, had packed up the show's apparatus and shipped it back to New York.

Somehow he missed the bronze coffin, though, and Houdini's body was placed in it for his final trip home.

Every major newspaper in the United States headlined Houdini's death. On the morning of November 4, almost two thousand people packed the Elks Club near Times Square for his funeral.

Rabbi Bernard Drachman, who had helped out Houdini's struggling father so many years before by buying *The Codes of Maimonides* from him, was one of two rabbis who conducted the service in Hebrew and English.

A past president of the Society of American Magicians broke a wand in half as members chanted these words:

"The curtain has at last been rung down. The wand is broken. God touched him with a wondrous gift and our brother made use of it. Now the wand is broken."

Houdini was buried, as he had directed, alongside his beloved mother. He also directed that his mother's letters to him be placed in a black bag and serve as the pillow that would hold his head throughout eternity.

A few days after the funeral, while going through his personal effects, Bess found his last letter to her.

"Sweetheart, when you read this I will be dead," he had written. "Heart, do not grieve; I shall be at rest by the side of my beloved parents, and wait for you always — remember! I loved only two women in my life; my mother and my wife. Yours, in Life, Death, and Ever After."

Bess, who had almost never been parted from the man she had fallen in love with thirty-two years before, said simply, "The world will never know what I have lost."

EPILOGUE

In 1928, a young Spiritualist minister named Arthur Ford conducted a séance with Bess. The first word that came through his mouth, supposedly from Houdini, was "Rosabelle." A second séance brought forth the word "believe."

Bess said, "I have gotten the message I have been waiting for from my beloved . . ."

But later there were charges that Ford was a fraud who had somehow learned of the message beforehand, and Bess decided that Houdini hadn't spoken to her after all. But she kept hoping and attended séances every Halloween through 1936, when she finally declared, "Houdini hasn't come. I am now convinced that he will never be able to come through. . . . My last hope is gone."

But every Halloween, magicians throughout the United States celebrate National Magic Day by holding séances to try and contact Houdini.

The man who spent a lifetime defying death continues to defy it decades after his passing. His legend is stronger than ever, and his name has become such a familiar part of the language that it is used every day.

Anyone who does something that seems impossible, from making a great catch in a ball game to squeezing out of a tight spot, is called a "Houdini."

His feats continue to amaze and puzzle people, even though he explained most of them. For instance, magicians continue to debate exactly how the Vanishing Elephant trick was done, just as they did in 1918 when the laughing Houdini told them, "Even the elephant doesn't know how it is done."

The mystery, courage, and controversy that were part of Houdini's life as a performer have helped turn him into a legend. It is hard to say exactly why people are still so fascinated by the man and his exploits, but psychoanalyst Bernard C. Meyer has perhaps come closest to explaining it.

"Whether he was hanging by his feet from the cornice of a tall building . . . buried six feet below the ground, or plunging from a bridge into the chill waters below," Meyer wrote in *Houdini: A Mind in Chains*, "he was not merely playing for publicity, as many people believed; he was living out a dream, an imagined horror that guided the sudden and unforeseen twists and turns of his strange existence . . ."

BIBLIOGRAPHY

Books

Brandon, Ruth. The Life and Many Deaths of Harry Houdini. NY: Random House, 1993.

Christopher, Milbourne. Houdini: The Untold Story. NY: Pocket Books, 1976.

Gibson, Walter B. Houdini's Escapes: Prepared From Houdini's Private Notebooks and Memoranda. NY: Bantam Books, 1976.

Gresham, William Lindsay. Houdini: The Man Who Walked Through Walls. NY: Macfadden Books, 1967.

Henning, Doug, with Charles Reynolds. Houdini: His Legend and His Magic. NY: Times Books, 1977.

Kellock, Harold. Houdini: His Life-Story by Harold Kellock from the Recollections and Documents of Beatrice Houdini. NY: Harcourt, Brace & Company, 1928.

Menninger, Karl A. Man Against Himself. NY: Harcourt, Brace & World, Inc., 1938.

Meyer, Bernard C., M.D. Houdini, A Mind in Chains: A Psychoanalytic Portrait. NY: E.P. Dutton & Co., 1976.

Silverman, Kenneth. Houdini!!! The Career of Erich Weiss. NY: HarperPerennial, 1996.

Williams, Beryl, and Epstein, Samuel. The Great Houdini: Magician Extraordinary. NY: Julian Messner, 1966.

Wood, Adam. The Importance of Harry Houdini. San Diego: Lucent Books, 1996.

Periodicals

Bragman, Louis J., M.D. "Houdini Escapes from Reality." The Psychoanalytic Review (October 1929). pp. 404–407.

"Harry Houdini." The National Cyclopaedia of American Biography, Vol. XXII (1932). p. 79.

Silverman, Kenneth. "Harry Houdini." American National Biography, Vol. 11 (1999). pp. 247–249.

Van Doren, Charles, and Robert McHenry. Webster's American Biographies (1974). pp. 509–510.

Zolotow, Maurice. "He Escaped from Everything but Mother." New York Times Book Review, Section 7 (March 23, 1969). pp. 7, 27–28.

Newspapers

"Doctors Attending Houdini Fear He Is Beyond Their Aid." The New York Times, October 27, 1926. p. 1.

"Harry Houdini Dies After Operations." The New York Times, November 1, 1926. p. 1.

"Houdini Exposes Fake Spiritualists in Talk at Van Curler Theatre." Schenectady Gazette (New York), October 15, 1926. p. 26.

"Houdini's Injury Not Serious, Will Be Here." Schenectady Gazette (New York), October 13, 1926. p. 21.

"Houdini's New Trick: Escapes from Huge Can of Water After Being Locked in Chest." The New York Times, July 3, 1912. p. 11.

INDEX